IMAGES *of our Past*

The

DOMINION ATLANTIC RAILWAY

1894–1994

GARY W. NESS

NIMBUS
PUBLISHING LTD

Nimbus Publishing Limited
3731 Mackintosh St, Halifax, NS B3K 5A5
(902) 455-4286 nimbus.ca

Printed and bound in Canada
NB1151

Cover photo: Final years of steam, c. 1957, Kentville. Harold Bailey Bob Bishop was on the window seat and John Morrison, the locomotive foreman from the roundhouse, was in the gangway when this photo was taken in the Kentville yard. Assigned to the DAR in 1957, this CPR D10 was one of only a few steamers that lingered after the CPR dieselized the line in August 1956. No. 1027 was retained, along with other Ten-wheelers Nos. 1046, 1077, and 1092, and Pacifics Nos. 2209 and 2501. Nos. 1027 and 2501 were the last to be sent to the scrap line at Kentville in the summer of 1961.
Clearly visible in the open doorway of the car shop was the 1958 Pontiac station wagon that the DAR used as a hi-rail inspection car after 1957. A picture of this vehicle is found on page 108; although distant, one can see the car-top rack that was being installed to transport bulky materials.

Cover and interior design: Jenn Embree

Library and Archives Canada Cataloguing in Publication

Ness, Gary W., author
The Dominion Atlantic Railway : 1894-1994 / Gary W. Ness.

Includes bibliographical references.
Issued in print and electronic formats.
ISBN 978-1-77108-168-9 (pbk.).--ISBN 978-1-77108-169-6 (html)

 1. Dominion Atlantic Railway—History. 2. Dominion Atlantic Railway—History--Pictorial works. 3. Railroads—Nova Scotia—Annapolis River Valley—History. 4. Railroads—Nova Scotia—Annapolis River Valley—History—Pictorial works. I. Title.

HE2810.D7N48 2014   385.09716'3   C2014-903193-9
                                        C2014-903194-7

Nimbus Publishing acknowledges the financial support for its publishing activities from the Government of Canada through the Canada Book Fund (CBF) and the Canada Council for the Arts, and from the Province of Nova Scotia through Film & Creative Industries Nova Scotia. We are pleased to work in partnership with Film & Creative Industries Nova Scotia to develop and promote our creative industries for the benefit of all Nova Scotians.

MIX
Paper from responsible sources
FSC www.fsc.org FSC® C103113

CONTENTS

THE DOMINION ATLANTIC RAILWAY

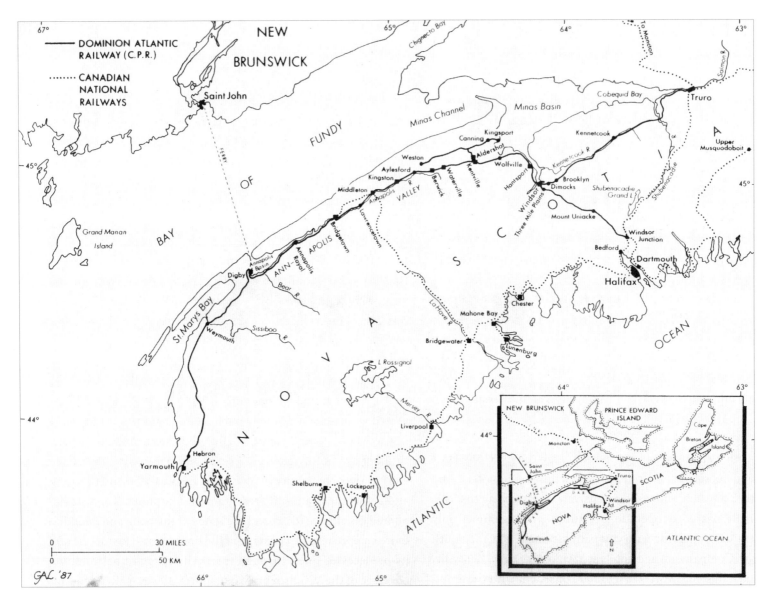

CREDIT: GEOFF A. LESTER

PREFACE

THE DOMINION ATLANTIC RAILWAY (DAR) WAS A SMALL, LOCAL RAILWAY REACHING FROM HALIFAX TO Yarmouth, Nova Scotia, by way of the Annapolis Valley and along the Bay of Fundy shoreline. Despite its size, it was very well known for beautiful seaside scenes and also had a reputation for the spit and polish of its trains and offering travel in first-class style. The practice of naming locomotives in its early years added to its charm, while the continued use of steam locomotives for an extended period after their disappearance elsewhere in North America was a draw in the 1950s.

The public perception of the line as a proud part of the famous Canadian Pacific Railway (CPR) system added mystique to the DAR. CPR takeovers, like most railway takeovers, tended to result in absorption and a subsequent loss of identity. Contrary to the trend, the DAR retained its independence and its own distinct identity, while still being part of the CPR system. In many ways, though, the DAR was a reflection of its owner. Advertising of the DAR often portrayed the company as part of a total transportation system with a strong focus on tourism. Like the CPR, the DAR owned and operated trains, ships, trucks, buses, and hotels. And the smaller subsidiary focused extensively on attracting tourists. For example, passenger operations featured special summer-only tourist trains connecting with company steamships at Yarmouth and Digby. Company-owned hotels at Yarmouth, Digby, Kentville, and Halifax hosted guests in a manner consistent with the grand CPR style of its world-renowned hotels.

Also like the CPR, the DAR became involved in developing tourist destinations, including parks. For instance, most of the early development of the Grand-Pré National Historic Site was due to the DAR. The use of historically important names to identify locomotives is presented in the Appendix.

The decision to write another DAR book occurred a long time ago. My collection of DAR photographs grew following some earlier publications, as people contacted me about their collections of negatives and prints. Often the images were the works of their fathers or grandfathers and had never been seen by anyone but the photographers. The wonderful work of these unheralded photographers needed to be shown. And of course, I have always enjoyed the research associated with a new photograph; discovering the stories associated with the images is fun.

When Nimbus managing editor Patrick Murphy and I first spoke, he suggested a large book with many new pictures integrated with some previously published images that would have revised and updated captions. The book would rely on what I think of as photo vignettes, a series of images with associated stories. The opportunity to revise and update the earlier captions, along with the chance to present many new pictures and stories offered the chance to expand the scope of the book and include a more comprehensive coverage of the line's overall history—from its predecessor lines, through the DAR era, and finally adding coverage of the Windsor and Hantsport Railway—all in one volume. The opportunity was irresistible, and the vague thoughts of another book and my rather slow, sporadic progress turned into steadfast commitment to complete the project.

This volume tends to follow a timeline from older images through to recent times. I have expanded the early histories and included the rosters of the predecessor lines; they were so intertwined with the DAR that ignoring them was impossible. The same is true about the Windsor and Hantsport Railway: there needed to be coverage of the DAR successor. And of course, there was a lot more to say about the DAR itself, from its period of growth to its decline.

The captions are shorter, but more stories and other information could be incorporated by collating and presenting roster and technical information in several captions and in appendices. Most importantly, a continued emphasis on the size and quality of photographs was achieved.

My love of trains began in childhood in Exeter, Ontario, where a plume of approaching smoke summoned us to run to see the daily branch-line train. This was in addition to visits to grandparents in Allandale, Ontario, where a busy train yard was just up Essa Road from their home. Best of all, my grandfather's two sisters were married to Canadian National Railway (CNR) engineers who drove the passenger trains out of Allandale, a division point where big CNR locomotives were watered at the stand-pipe while crews changed. My great-uncles took me up into those steam locomotive cabs on numerous occasions. An indelible memory from those very early childhood years was being frightened when one of them opened the firebox's butterfly doors to reveal a white-hot fire—the fires of hell—at my face level. I still recall what those trains and that station looked like.

I have always stopped to watch trains, and when we moved to Wolfville in 1976, it was impossible to ignore the daily freight and passenger trains that ran through town. The DAR tracks were immediately behind the Acadia University building where I worked, and the horns blowing for crossings were easily heard in my office. I also encountered trains along Wolfville's back routes to the dykes on my daily noon-hour runs.

An interest in the photographic history of the DAR started while walking to and from the university. The photo opposite of Pacific No. 2500 beginning to accelerate from a stop at the Wolfville station was prominently displayed in the front window of the (Lee) Johnston Insurance Company office across from the fire station. When I finally worked up the nerve to ask, the photograph was not for sale, but I admired it in passing and thought about it for several years before Mr. Johnston unexpectedly gave it to me.

All I knew about it was that it was an interesting Canadian Pacific Railway (CPR) train, but I was intrigued. I quickly learned that Edgar DeWolfe was an avid train fan who took a lot of photographs of DAR trains. He was known to meet the trains regularly, and I suspected that the print was his work. I also pieced together some details about the image, such as the position of the freight shed at the left and that the station platform ended at the freight shed. It was also clear that the train has just begun to move forward since the plume of steam and smoke is quite dark and the shape of the plume shows a distinctive spread from one explosive chuff—the result of the throttle being opened moments earlier.

Wolfville, c. 1940. EDGAR DEWOLFE / GARY NESS COLLECTION

ACKNOWLEDGEMENTS

Many people have helped me to explore and learn about the photographic history of the Dominion Atlantic Railway. It has been a wonderful experience to see their photographs, to hear their stories about the trains, and to learn some new details that filled in a missing piece or opened new lines of inquiry and exploration. Many gave freely of their time to share stories and willingly contributed images and historical documents. Others helped with technical matters, such as reproducing or fixing damaged photographs, and making technical drawings or maps. And still others allowed me access to the railway to photograph the trains. I enjoyed meeting and working with every one of them since I began this exploration in the late seventies. And I thank them all for making this collection of pictures and stories possible.

The photographer's name appears below their photograph whenever possible. I also note the source for images, usually a private collection, when it is known. The citations include the photographer's name first, followed by a slash, followed by the source(s) (i.e., collection). When the photographer provided me with their photograph, only the photographer's name appears.

For some older images the name of the photographer is not known; it was very disappointing when a photographer could not be given credit. If anyone knows who these "missing" photographers are, please let me know. It is important to credit photographers for their contributions to preserving our history.

The following list is long, and I hope that I have not missed anyone. A sincere thank you to the photographers and collectors who provided images and information for the captions: Harold Bailey, Wendell Lemon, Ken MacDonald, Edgar DeWolfe, Charlie Hatfield, Bill Linley, A. Ross Harrison, Robert Sandusky, Jim O'Donnell, George Bishop, Jim Shaughnessy, Dale Wilson, Harold A. Jenkins, Bob Brooks, Ian Donaldson, L. G. Swain, J. C. M. Hayward, Robert Taylor, Roger Robinson, Fred Sankoff, William A. Stephens, A. L. Hardy, J. Norman Lowe, George Parks, R. Robinson, J. P. R., P. Bishop, Wendy Elliott, Stephen Slipp, Paul and Betty Cleveland, John Riddell, Bob Morrison, William Lightle, David DeWolfe, David Stephens, Dick George, Al Paterson, Dorothy and Joe Taylor, James Walder, John D. Williams, Louis Comeau, Andrea Lynn, Baldwin Locomotive Works, Keith Sirman, and Harold K. Vollrath.

Another deeply felt thank you to the DAR and WHRC railway people, including the Humphrey Club members who shared the stories that bring the pictures to life: Cyril White Sr., Harley Cochrane, Albert (Shine) Manning, Harry Balsor, Clyde Earle, Vernon Corey, Don Pearl, Earle MacLeod, Don Hiltz, Arthur Forcey, Maurice (Bud) Sanford, Earle MacLeod, Vincent Coxhead, John DeWolfe, Gerald Balsor, Carl Bancroft, Bob Bishop, John Gee, Carter Smith, Sheldon Wambolt, Gerry Parks, Leon Barron, John Clark, Bob Clark, Ron Campbell, Ken Beyea, Gary Fitzgerald, Carl Forsyth, Robert Taylor, Malcolm Taylor, John D. Williams, Willis Forsyth, John Harnish, Gary Wentzell, Allan Russell, Mike Smith, Barry Buchanan, Bev Buchanan, Clayton Benjamin, Blair Smith, Wayne Smith, Gilbert Forsyth, Fred Wilcox, Allan Smith, Elwood Dillman, John Hughes, Peter Laing, Floyd Russell, Richard (Dick) Pineo, Peter Johnson, and Lawrence Anthony. A very special thanks is owed to Jim Murray who agreed to write first-hand stories about his experiences driving DAR trains and to Bob Schmidt, WHRC owner, and Jim Taylor, WHRC manager, who granted access to photograph the railway.

A number of noted historians and historical groups also

provided images, documents, and invaluable help with detailed information: Bruce Chapman, Garnet Clark, Bob Boudreau, Carl Riff, Dan Conlin, Garnet Brown, Donnie Foster, Jim Simmons, Stuart McCann, Larry Boner and the Nova Scotia Department of Government Services, Ruby Kelly and the Musquodoboit Railway Museum, Bria Stokesbury and the Kings Historical Society, the National Railway Museum (York, UK), CP Photographic Services, CPR Archivist Omer Lavallée, and Nancy Battet and Jim Shields of CPR Archives. Thank you.

Still others provided technical support that added appreciably to the final outcome. Thanks to Doug Phillips, Geoff Lester (for the map), BRMNA associates Don Bain, Martin Booth, and Bill Cruickshanks, Gerry Raymond and Bill Mills of Fundy Gypsum, Larry Keddy of Lark Photographic Services, Jocelyn Hatt (photo restoration), and Thomas Bagley (technical drawing).

Thanks also to the Mud Creek Boys, the audiences at our train shows, and the DAR fans who never stopped asking when the next book was coming.

A special thank you to Patrick Murphy, who patiently worked with me to publish this.

And a heartfelt thank you to my wife, Jan, whose support has made this, and everything I have done, possible.

A NOTE ON SOURCES

For those interested in a detailed history of the promotion, building, and early operations of the DAR predecessor railways, Marguerite Woodworth's 1936 book *History of the Dominion Atlantic Railway*, and William Clarke's book *Clarke's History of the Earliest Railways in Nova Scotia*, are excellent resources.

Although long out of print, Woodworth's book is still readily available. A copy of Clarke's undated book printed just after 1925, however, will require a more deliberate quest.

Newspaper reporter Henry Bruce Jefferson published numerous detailed articles on the history of Nova Scotia railroads, which appeared in the *Chronicle-Herald* from 1957 to 1961 under the pen name J. B. King. Those articles were laden with interesting stories and were very well researched.

Carl Riff deserves special mention. He has compiled old newspaper clippings, copies of reports, collections of old documents, and records of "stuff" related to the DAR into files. He has over six hundred fact-laden pages and he continues to search further.

Omer Lavallée was CPR's corporate archivist and historian. His 1985 book *Canadian Pacific Steam Locomotives* is an outstanding resource if you are interested in details about all aspects of steam development, technology, roster information, and overall history.

Murray W. Dean and David B. Hanna's 1981 book *Canadian Pacific Diesel Locomotives* is the diesel companion to Omer Lavallée's steam locomotive book.

My collection of DAR public and employee timetables, pamphlets, booklets, and official documents and reports about the railway were critical. The DAR DPI (Dominion Atlantic Railway Digital Preservation Initiative) website was also a wealth of information.

The annual *Canadian Trackside Guides* produced by the Bytown Railway Society were very useful for research about modern-day rosters.

HAVE YOU SEEN A STEAM LOCOMOTIVE WITH A GREAT CLOUD OF EXHAUST ISSUING FROM ITS STACK AND wondered how it works? I did, and this is a simplified version of what I discovered. A DAR steam locomotive burned coal (1) to heat water (2) in its boiler (3). The burning coal (4) was spread across a grate (5) in the firebox (6). This grate had holes through which ashes and cinders dropped into an ashpan (7). The grate also allowed airflow (8) upward to the fire. Hot fumes and smoke (9) from the fire were drawn upwards around a brick arch (10) before entering the boiler tubes (11), which ran forward through the boiler to the smoke box (12). The temperature of the crown sheet (13) at the top of the firebox was the hottest place in the boiler; water on top of it was over 400°F and most steam (14) was created there. However the hot gases and smoke in the boiler tubes heated the surrounding water as well. Steam collected at the top of the boiler above the water level (15) and in the steam dome (16). Steam was under considerable pressure, up to 250 psi (pounds per square inch), in the enclosed space. The engineer used the throttle (17) to open and close a valve (18) inside the steam dome; the valve admitted high-pressure steam to a dry pipe (19), which directed it to the pistons. En route, super-heater coils (20) in the upper portion of the boiler raised the temperature of the steam further to prevent condensation of steam inside the piston. (Liquid water was not compressible and interfered with piston function; it had to be blown out of the pistons periodically.) The upper piston was a valve (21) that moved back and forth admitting steam first behind the piston

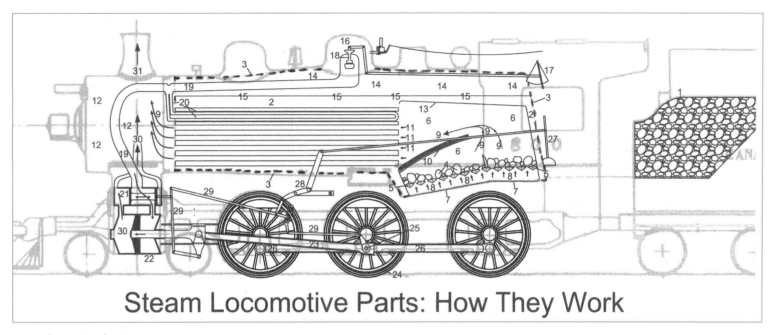

Steam Locomotive Parts: How They Work

Steam locomotive function. OMER LAVALLÉE (CANADIAN PACIFIC ARCHIVES) & THOMAS BAGLEY

(22) then in front of it to create push–pull forces on the drive rod (23). The drive rod was attached to the drive wheel (24) at a point that was off-centre (25). This applied an eccentric force to the drive wheel and it turned. The side rod (26) transmitted the force to the other drive wheels to increase tractive forces.

The engineer could adjust the valve above the piston for forward and backward movement; in this case, a Johnson bar (27) and connecting rods (28) linked to the valve positioned it. The valve also automatically controlled the timing of the flow of steam to the piston by way of an intricate series of rods, the valve gear (29). When the locomotive was moving, high-pressure steam moved the piston to its limit, then the valve was moved automatically to admit steam on the other side of the piston head. The pressurized steam that was driving the piston moments ago was then exhausted (30) upwards into the smoke box and up the smokestack (31) with a great chuff. This steam exhaust created a Venturi effect in the smoke box that drew smoke forcefully through the boiler tubes into the smoke box. This, in turn, caused the fire to draw more air upward through the grate under the coal, which then burned more intensely and much hotter with the rapid passage of air.

Chapter 1

THE PREDECESSOR LINES

THE WINDSOR BRANCH

JOSEPH (JOE) HOWE WAS STILL ONE YEAR AWAY FROM BEING ELECTED TO THE NOVA SCOTIA HOUSE OF Assembly and the beginning of his long, illustrious political career, when, in 1835, he made a horseback tour of the Annapolis Valley. As the owner of and a journalist for his newspaper, the *Novascotian,* he had toured many parts of the province and realized that transportation was a key to future development; he became an early champion of railway building in Nova Scotia.

Upon his return to Halifax, he recruited a powerful ally, Dr. Charles Tupper, to his cause and began to publish articles about the need for a line to the Annapolis Valley. He recognized that the Valley held the most productive farmland in the province, but the key market for the crops was not Halifax, it was Saint John, New Brunswick. The six- or seven-hour trip across the province on a

terrible road was a considerable obstacle for passengers; freight wagons took days. The numerous schooners that frequented the ports along the Bay of Fundy were more reliable and accessible for transporting farm produce to markets bordering the Bay of Fundy, and particularly to the large port of Saint John. Howe knew a railway could shorten the cross-province trip between Halifax and Windsor to two hours, serving to make Halifax a preferred market, but more importantly, forging a critical link within Nova Scotia.

However, it was not until 1845 that the political will emerged to engage in railway building in the province and this was centred on a line linking Halifax to Quebec City. Ironically, one of the early proposals for that route was from Halifax to Windsor, thence to a point on the Bay of Fundy, and finally to Saint John to connect to an existing line that could connect to Quebec City. This was quickly dismissed due to critical flaws. The route was deemed to need uninterrupted service at all times and in all seasons, and it had to be secure for transport of troops and war materials; the segment across the Bay of Fundy met none of these criteria.

Political wrangling and the search for financial backing for railway construction in Nova Scotia continued for almost twenty years before the provincial government passed a motion in 1854 to build the Nova Scotia Railway (NSR) in three parts, one piece of which was the connection of Halifax to the Bay of Fundy. The primary focus remained the Intercolonial Railway (ICR) to Quebec, but a line to the Valley assured that—even if the commitment to build was only as far as Windsor—the Windsor Branch finally would be built.

The province immediately set about building the line westward from Halifax and had contracts by late 1854 for the work to the junction where the lines to the Annapolis Valley and Truro split. Interestingly, the decision then was made to begin building the Windsor line first. Work proceeded slowly, hampered by cost overruns and lack of funds, the sinking of a ship carrying building materials, the wreck of a locomotive, disputes between builders and contractors, and so on. The line was not ready by June 1857, the agreed completion date, and would not be ready for another year.

On June 3, 1858, the first official train departed Halifax for Windsor amidst great fanfare not orchestrated by the Conservative Government of the day, which had opposed building the stretch of railway from the start. The Liberals reportedly stole the day. There were decorations at stations, on the train, and along the line. A public holiday was declared in Halifax and church bells in the city rang at 5:30 AM to rouse people for the 7:30 AM departure. Three hundred leading Liberals filled the train. The public turned out in large numbers along the line or at station stops to see the train, which arrived at 11:00 AM in Windsor. Local Liberals, who hosted festivities there, decorated the station extensively.

The day was marred only by a serious derailment of a passenger train on the NSR Halifax–Truro run. The locomotive went over an embankment and its crew was badly scalded, but the passenger train stayed on the track. There was no loss of life.

J. B. King noted that there were three firsts associated with that day's celebrations: a newspaper cameraman documented the event in daguerreotypes; a new Nova Scotia flag (which resembled the present design but had a centrepiece featuring the arms of the province, not the red lion and gold shield) was unveiled; and a section of the Commons, now the Wanderers Grounds, was presented to the Halifax Cricket Club.

Thereafter, the train was well used by interested sightseers and passengers travelling to small ports along the coast in Nova Scotia, New Brunswick, and across the border, but especially to Saint John, Portland, Boston, and Upper Canada; however, railway-steamship connections to the latter services were problematic. The steamships could not stay moored for long at the Windsor dock, and the trains were often late due to problems loading and unloading freight while en route to Windsor. Ferries often sailed without passengers. Nonetheless, in the first year of operation, passengers were using the service.

The movement of wagonloads of farm produce, which were loaded onto flatcars for shipment to Halifax, proved to be unprofitable. Low tariffs had been used initially to attract business, but the volume of traffic did not increase as hoped.

Vernon Smith statue unveiling, Wolfville, 2014.
STEVEN SLIPP

✍ **ON SEPTEMBER 21,** 2013, Vernon Smith, the builder, engineer, and first general manager of the Windsor and Annapolis Railway was immortalized in a bronze statue situated in the Waterfront Park in Wolfville. The statue is the work of Ruth Abernethy, a noted Canadian sculptor. The statue was commissioned by Smith's grandson, Allen Eaves, and was unveiled in a special ceremony shown here. A crowd of over two hundred people gathered to witness the event, which included the unveiling ceremony, a reception, and a "train show" entitled the Dominion Atlantic Railway, an Evening of Pictures, Stories and Songs with Gary Ness and the Mud Creek Boys (Peter Williams, Ian Spooner, "JP" Huang, and Sean Myles).

The group surrounding the statue had just unveiled it. On the far side, from the right are: Ruth Abernethy (sculptor), Jim and Beth Wilson (Castaway Foundry), and Terry Hennigar. On the near side (with their backs to the camera), from the right are: Gary Ness, Bob Stead (former mayor of Wolfville), Jeff Cantwell (mayor of Wolfville), and obscured behind him, Allen Eaves, grandson of Vernon Smith and the donor of this wonderful piece of public art.

The statue features Vernon Smith overlooking a large map of the area to the east of Wolfville, spread on a large bronze trestle table. The Smith statue's gaze is fixed on the section of the Windsor and Annapolis Railway that was damaged by the Saxby Gale (pages 132 and 133).

Moreover, loading and unloading horses and wagons onto flatcars wreaked havoc with timetables, especially when another flatcar had to be added to the train. Sweeping changes were introduced, and by the end of 1860 the railway was operating somewhat more efficiently. However, succeeding governments continued to mismanage the line's finances. The line was unprofitable and suffered from deferred maintenance, particularly since the priority had been shifted to the Truro line as the likelihood of Confederation peaked.

THE WINDSOR AND ANNAPOLIS RAILWAY (W&AR)

The concept of a western extension through the Annapolis Valley had been discussed since Joe Howe first published his 1835 vision for a Nova Scotia Railway, which included the idea of a line to Yarmouth via Windsor. Talk about this westward extension increased steadily once the intention to build the Nova Scotia Railway's Windsor Branch was announced, and the "On to Annapolis" movement grew when the line to Windsor was opened in June 1858. However, at that time the NSR line to Truro was the government's immediate priority, until the lobbying became so intense that the government approved a motion to implement the portion of the 1854 Railway Act that required the building of a line west of Windsor. But the call for tenders produced little response because funding was scarce and the building of the ICR had taken centre stage.

Although Charles Tupper, now the provincial secretary, lobbied to have the western extension included in the ICR plans, this never happened because a tendered bid arrived from civil engineer T. T. Vernon Smith and a group of investors in England. Meetings and negotiations led to the signing of a letter of agreement, dated October 25, 1865, to begin construction of a line between Windsor and Annapolis by May 1866, one year prior to Confederation. It was to be completed within two years. Unfortunately, a financial crisis in England resulted in bankruptcy of Smith's group of investors, and the official start date passed with no obvious work done. Smith had hired surveyors and contractors, some from Nova Scotia and others who came from England, to do preparatory work before groundbreaking. All of them, including Smith, had amassed considerable debts and faced serious legal penalties.

Smith and Tupper—separately—went to England committed to finance and build the railway. Another contractor was secured; Smith and Tupper and the firm of Punchard, Barry & Clark signed an agreement requiring the builders to also operate the line. Construction was to start by January 1, 1867, and be completed by December 1, 1869. Most importantly, the W&AR was given running rights over the Windsor Branch and the NSR line into Halifax.

Smith paid off debts to proceed, reassembled his workers, and began on schedule building at Hantsport. According to Marguerite Woodworth's *History of the Dominion Atlantic Railway*, Smith was a man on a mission; he was promoted to general manager of the line, all the while continuing to fulfill his role as the engineer overseeing construction, which went ahead against all obstacles, including winter, financial difficulties, and geographic challenges, such as the Bay of Fundy's very high tides and wide river estuaries. He also managed and supervised the day-to-day minutiae and operations of the line: from hiring

Early W&AR scene, Kentville. KINGS HISTORICAL SOCIETY COLLECTION

↝ **THIS IS AN EARLY** image of the W&AR Kentville station area. Luckily, a few other views of that area exist, possibly taken by the same photographer; the quality of the image suggests that a top-quality lens was used, and few people would have had one. J. B. King used those images in his newspaper articles, in which he identified the key buildings in the scenes. Those published images were what Alex McNab, the provincial engineer, would have seen in his 1873 provincial government-sponsored investigation into the state of the W&AR, with the looming possibility that the government would sell the line to a company that could repay W&AR debts.

It is impossible to be certain about the photographer, the date of this third image, or the reason for creating it. Regardless, we know from McNab's records and from King's articles that the large building at the right, on the south side of the rails, was the original Windsor and Annapolis Railway station and headquarters. Just visible behind it to the right were the outdoor toilets, accessed by a covered passageway. Across the tracks was the freight shed and at the far left in the distance was the car repair shop. Beside the station and hidden by the train was the woodyard, with piles of fuel. Note the absence of any town buildings in the background; this, too, suggests a very early date.

running crews, station and office personnel, to production of timetables, forms, and advertisements.

The first W&AR passenger train ran from Annapolis to Wolfville on June 26, 1869, and on August 19, 1869, the line was declared officially open, although the bridges across the Avon and Gaspereaux Rivers were not complete.

Descriptions of the event indicate everything that could be decorated was adorned. The public flocked to the stations, or at least saw the passing trains, and enjoyed a day of bands and speeches. The ceremonies began in Halifax, from which a large group of VIPs left on a special ICR train at 8:00 AM. Arriving in Windsor, they boarded coaches (buses) for transport to Grand-Pré, where they were greeted with more pomp and ceremony before boarding a W&AR train led by a highly decorated EVANGELINE—now painted in the colours that would characterize the W&AR and later the DAR: magenta, gold, and black. This westbound train stopped in Wolfville before proceeding to Kentville, where a second eastbound train from Annapolis arrived shortly thereafter. It, too, carried VIPs and had a similar ceremonial departure and trip. The VIPs were treated to more ceremonies and hosted at a sumptuous banquet. The guests were returned to their respective points of departure late that same day.

Construction of the Windsor–Avonport section continued, with passengers moved by bus across the Grand-Pré–Windsor gap. It was almost finished when the Saxby Gale of October 4, 1869, hit the Valley. Farms were damaged and crops destroyed. Flooding wrecked the twenty miles of railway between Kentville and Horton. The storm lasted for hours, and each storm-driven wave of the extreme high tides did more harm. Dykes failed early in the Wolfville area, allowing the tide to erode the track ballast and rip trestles apart. Worse yet, subsequent high tides in October and November undid repair efforts. In spite of this, Smith's railway was completed on December 18, 1869, only two weeks behind schedule—a Herculean effort.

However, the railway was experiencing financial difficulties, and to make matters worse, there was an unexpected surge in freight traffic that backed up in Annapolis, awaiting export to Saint John and eastern United States ports. Moreover, initial passenger traffic using the Annapolis ferries increased, which was quite promising until the Nova Scotia government subsidized ferries running from Windsor and Halifax to Saint John, after which traffic declined. The W&AR limped along, barely staying solvent and in decline.

In 1871 an agreement with the federal government was reached that set out the terms by which the W&AR would operate the Dominion government–owned Windsor Branch and have running rights over ICR rails into Halifax, the latter being a condition in the contract to build the W&AR. On January 1, 1872, the first through-train ran from Halifax to Annapolis. However, the Windsor Branch was also in need of repair, and this arrangement did little to solve the W&AR's financial problems. The British owners on the W&AR appointed Peter Innis as accountant. His sole job was to control expenditures. In 1872 Vernon Smith, a frustrated engineer at heart, left to build the Western Counties Railway from Annapolis to Yarmouth. Innis became the next general manager.

After 1872 the W&AR's prospects improved slowly. Passenger and freight revenues increased, although almost all the income went into operations and the seemingly endless need for repairs.

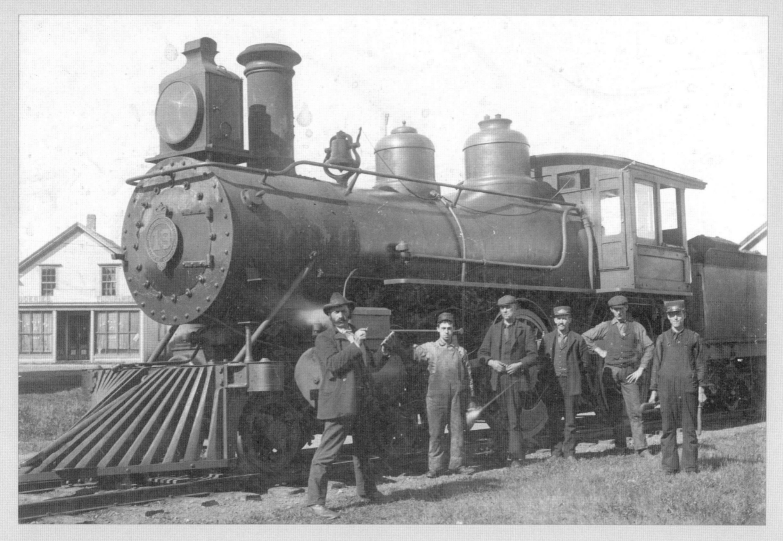

DAR No. 19 OBERON. GARY NESS COLLECTION

❧ **DAR NO. 19 OBERON** originated as W&AR No. 15 and was still a good example of how it looked on the W&AR. The original link and pin coupler (page 15), the slatted wood cowcatcher, and the old kerosene headlight were all still present. Built in 1893, it had a short life after the DAR was transferred to CPR control. It was among the first small 4-4-0s to be scrapped, in 1920.

The W&AR was unable to pay the Dominion government's rental fees for use of the Windsor Branch and hovered on the brink of defaulting on their contract, in which case the W&AR would lose control of the Windsor Branch. On May 23, 1873, the Dominion government approved a motion to pass over control of the Windsor Branch to any company that would build a line from Annapolis to Yarmouth, and soon after began planning to convert the Windsor Branch to standard gauge (4 feet 8.5 inches) to be consistent with its own ICR. The W&AR had been built to broad gauge (5 feet 6 inches).

Talks continued without success, but in 1875 when the gauge-changeover date was imminent, the government suddenly agreed to waive the W&AR debt if the W&AR would standard gauge their railway by July 1 of that year. The government also agreed to swap broad-gauge locomotives and freight and passenger trucks for equal numbers of standard-gauge equipment. They also included written approval for the W&AR to continue to operate the Windsor Branch. Naturally, the W&AR owners agreed.

The gauge was changed over from Windsor to Annapolis in ten hours. A few days prior, spikes had been driven in a line along the sleepers (ties) exactly 4 feet 8.5 inches over from the south rail. Then spikes were drawn at every second tie along the inner edge of the north rail. For the actual changeover, gangs of extra men moved the rail across and spiked it in place. New standard gauge trucks (wheel sets), provided by the Dominion government, arrived in Kentville in time to switch many of them just prior to the rail alterations; the replacement locomotives were also ready to begin work.

By the end of 1876, the W&AR's infrastructure had been upgraded and passenger usage was better; however, the heavy freight traffic that could benefit the line was unpredictable at best. The railway was not faring well financially. In 1877 the Dominion government took back control of the Windsor Branch and the associated rolling stock and passed control to the WCR.

Almost immediately, W&AR access to the Windsor Branch was blocked at both ends. A large tree was felled across the rails near Windsor. At the opposite end the switch to the Branch at Windsor Junction was locked and a locomotive was parked in the way. The Windsor Branch became known as the Eastern Division of the WCR.

Real acrimony followed, and the Windsor yard became a very unfriendly place to work. Halifax crews bringing WCR trains to and from Windsor met public resentment in the town. Worse yet, rival gangs prowled the Windsor yard, damaging the rival railway's equipment and quite often fighting during the night using such weapons as "borrowed" coupling links. (Page 15.)

Both companies adopted strategies of passive resistance and harassment, and the costs of operations increased greatly. Passengers and shippers were forced to deal with two competing companies at Windsor and again at Annapolis if their travels required it. At its worst, rather than interchanging loaded passenger cars and freight cars on a continuous rail connection joining the two railways, through passengers were forced to disembark and change trains, while all freight was moved between cars across a platform.

The W&AR went so far as to alter freight rates to divert freight traffic to ships rather than via the WCR-run Branch; special incentives to ship via Annapolis Royal and Windsor harbours were introduced. At the same time, because of the turmoil at Windsor and Annapolis Royal, the expenses of shipping

W&AR train, Windsor, 1891.
PAUL CLEVELAND COLLECTION

☞ **WINDSOR AND ANNAPOLIS** Railway (W&AR) locomotive No. 10 KENTVILLE was nearly new when an unknown photographer took this excellent shot in Windsor. KENTVILLE was acquired by the W&AR in 1891, the year that this photograph is believed to have been taken. Delivered as No. 10, it was renumbered to No. 12 when the DAR was formed in 1894. The name of the locomotive was retained after the merger. KENTVILLE had an historic role in the merger when it became the first "foreign" locomotive to run over the Annapolis Royal–Yarmouth section of the WCR, pulling a special train of DAR dignitaries to Yarmouth for the official takeover on October 1, 1894. The conductor, W. W. Clarke, went on to publish a wonderful little book, *Clarke's History of the Earliest Railways in Nova Scotia* (1926). His series of recollections and anecdotes has been described as a "Bluenose folklore classic" and is compulsory reading for fans of the DAR.

This eastbound passenger train appears to be standing on the main line in front of the freight house, which is partially visible at the left in front of the locomotive, and the Windsor station, seen above the first and second passenger cars. The station was unusual, having been built to standard ICR wooden station plans about 1881 by the Dominion government, which was running the Windsor Branch at the time. The large building at the right is the Dufferin Hotel, a famous Windsor landmark destroyed in the 1897 great fire, which burned a substantial portion of the downtown area.

increased alarmingly. For example, it cost fifty cents to ship a barrel of flour from Halifax to Bridgetown, but only twenty-three cents from Saint John, New Brunswick. Valley freight business was reverting to Saint John and away from Halifax.

Although the public was furious, problems continued until 1879, when the governing party changed once again and the Dominion government took back control of the Windsor Branch on the grounds that the WCR had not met the requirements of their agreement to operate the line. The W&AR resumed operating the Windsor Branch.

THE WESTERN COUNTIES RAILWAY (WCR)

Yarmouth was a thriving seaport when railway building began in Nova Scotia. It was ideally situated to have shipping access to the Bay of Fundy, the United States Eastern Seaboard and European ports; however, the three-hundred-kilometre trip to Halifax by stagecoach was arduous at best, and much slower by ship.

By the mid-1860s, it became obvious that the lines in the Valley could be used to advantage if a railway to Yarmouth was built, and four hundred Yarmouth residents petitioned the government to do so. At first, the petition was ignored, although Vernon Smith, general manager of the W&AR, had always felt that the W&AR should be extended to Yarmouth. He had maintained contact with the Yarmouth promoters, and in fact had told them that the W&AR would build the line. Of course, this was a contractual requirement of the original agreement for the W&AR to operate the Windsor Branch.

By 1870, with little real progress in building the WCR, it was apparent the W&AR would not fulfill that obligation. The provincial government created the Western Counties Railway Company to build the final piece of the western extension from Annapolis to Yarmouth. The company was granted money and lands to facilitate the work. Vernon Smith was listed as a shareholder in the WCR in 1871, and after resigning from the W&AR, he became chief engineer of the WCR in 1872.

The route of the line was controversial to say the least. Numerous factions argued to either place the line along the coast, particularly through their respective towns or inland for ready access to lumber and land for development. The final decision was a series of compromises, with the line meandering back and forth.

The haggling over which railway would operate the Windsor Branch continued, and until that could be resolved, construction would not start. Matters came to a critical point in 1873 with the Dominion government offering the Windsor Branch to the company that would build the line to Yarmouth; the WCR Company commenced work shortly afterwards. Smith's survey was completed in 1873, and sod was turned in Yarmouth and Digby in that same year. As mentioned, the Windsor Branch—and its running rights into Halifax—were turned over to the WCR with an important proviso that the Branch would be owned by the WCR when their line was completed from Annapolis to Yarmouth.

Work on the WCR line was costly and slow, and only nine miles of track were laid by late 1874. Short on finances, yet counting on revenue from the Windsor Branch, when the WCR proved unable to operate the Branch, the government reversed their decision and allowed the W&AR to continue to operate it. This action worsened the WCR's financial situation. Construction of the WCR was slowed further, until lobbying convinced the

WCR picnic excursion, Yarmouth, 1875. L. G. SWAIN / PAUL CLEVELAND COLLECTION

✍ **FROM 1957 TO** 1961 well-known journalist and railway historian H. B. Jefferson wrote numerous articles about early Nova Scotia railways; these appeared under the pseudonym J. B. King. One particularly entertaining anecdote, in a July 19, 1958, article, dealt with a large picnic excursion on the early WCR.

On May 11, 1875, at Yarmouth, twelve flatcars fitted with benches took an estimated twelve hundred "venturesome souls" for a "May Ride" and picnic. The train was decorated like a ship with numerous flags on the locomotive, 4-4-0 No. 2 PIONEER, and a long string of international naval code flags on the sides of the flatcars spelled "WCR YARMOUTH." The ensign was displayed on a staff affixed to the boxcar at the "stern."

A band seated along the centre of the train played "lively airs." The train eased slowly along the new, unballasted track to Pittman's Road, a distance of eight or nine miles to the picnic grounds where partygoers enjoyed dancing and picking wildflowers in the nearby woods.

PIONEER was fired with wood on this day, a fact that became only too obvious later. It was kept hot with a simmering wood fire for many hours until the locomotive whistle recalled the picnickers. The day's excitement was not over. The train was positioned on a slight uphill grade, and when the engineer opened the throttle the drivers slipped, causing a great draught of air to be sucked through the firebox and up the stack, spewing "bushels" of glowing embers over the entire length of the train. Flammables such as the women's parasols were instantly in flames. Fortunately, water from a nearby spring was available to extinguish any persistent fires.

Dominion government to reverse their decision once more. The Windsor Branch was handed over to the WCR, which was given until October 1879 to complete the WCR line or be in default.

The WCR immediately recommenced operation of the Windsor Branch; however, work on the WCR then languished until the government provided financing to complete the portion of the WCR line from Digby to Yarmouth. That agreement required the WCR to operate trains on the Yarmouth–Annapolis section and to provide steamship service via the Annapolis Basin from Annapolis to Digby, past what became known as the "Missing Link." The first Yarmouth–Digby train ran in August 1879, but when the government deemed the new WCR line to be unsafe, it ceded the Windsor Branch back to the W&AR on December 1, 1879.

Bitterly disappointed, the WCR Company focused efforts on their Digby–Yarmouth line, which was in dire need of upgrades to its infrastructure. While passengers and freight could move from Yarmouth to Halifax, much reduced speeds and an unreliable ferry–train connection across the Missing Link made the trip a significant challenge. Although annual statistics of that period show that passengers and shippers were using the new service, from the government's perspective the overall situation was untenable. Service through the Valley was not good with the W&AR and WCR in continuous conflict. And there was still the matter of completing the track across the Missing Link. A resolution was needed.

THE CORNWALLIS VALLEY RAILWAY

The lands north of Kentville were some of the most fertile in the province, and farming dominated the area. Initially people and farm goods moved by small ferries or wagon back and forth to W&AR trains at Kentville from Kingsport, but by 1887 it was clear to the residents that a rail line was essential if their area were to prosper. They obtained support from the W&AR and lobbied the provincial government, which quickly approved the formation of the Cornwallis Valley Railway Company in May 1887. The provincial government also provided funding and the land for the route.

There was some difference of opinion about whether Kentville or Middleton should be the terminus. Middleton had connections to the W&AR, but of more interest was the connection to the Nictaux and Atlantic Railway (N&AR), which ran across the province from Middleton to Bridgewater on Nova Scotia's South Shore. The N&AR would later become part of the ICR and ultimately the CNR.

The deciding factor was the willingness of the lines to take over and operate the Cornwallis Valley Railway (CVR) once it was built. The new W&AR Resident Manager, J. W. King, quietly and pre-emptively acted to ensure that it would reach Kentville. Work on the railway began in 1889 and was completed in December 1890. The W&AR leased the CVR facilities and equipment to operate their line, which was a success from the outset. The CVR immediately attracted steamships to its wharf at Kingsport and traffic on the line blossomed overnight—some of it at the expense of the W&AR line west of Kentville. The CVR was purchased by the W&AR in July 1892, two years before the DAR was formed.

Weymouth station, c. 1890s.

‱ **EVEN WITHOUT THE** prominently labelled cars in the train, it is immediately apparent that the photograph was taken on the WCR. The station is a classic WCR structure with the characteristic unique finials projecting upward from the roof ends and from the dormers. The three dormers on this station identify the site as Weymouth. Most other WCR stations had one dormer; only Weymouth had three. The small building at the left, behind the stack of lumber, was probably the outside toilet facilities common at that time. It was not unusual to find these small buildings linked to the main station by a covered passageway designed to protect passengers from the weather; however, that feature is not apparent in this view.

Coincidentally the locomotive was named WEYMOUTH and was No. 8 of the WCR. After amalgamation, it retained both name and number in DAR service. This photograph reveals a number of interesting features about WEYMOUTH. The headlight, normally mounted on the platform immediately in front of the smokestack, is missing. Obviously this train was scheduled to complete its run during daylight hours. The covering over the cowcatcher suggests the photograph was taken during a season when snow was expected; the covering assisted in snow removal and was installed in late autumn.

Train and ferry meet, Kingsport, 1911.
HAROLD BAILEY

 THE LADY SEATED comfortably on a convenient plank in the centre of this scene, shielded from the sun's intense rays by her parasol, was watching the operations during high tide at the government wharf in Kingsport. On this summer day in 1911, activity was particularly intense. In addition to the regular meeting of the train and the DAR steamship *Prince Albert*, there was construction work under way on the wharf. The wharf, built with its distal half projecting at a slight angle to the right, was being extended 140 feet. The logs on the beach in the foreground would serve as piles, while the lumber stacked on the wharf would form planking for the extensions to the wharf. The lighthouse, normally located at the end of the wharf, appears to be well short of that position in this

view. What may be a piledriver (seen beyond the twin masts of the *Prince Albert*) occupies the end of the wharf.

The DAR's Kingsport Subdivision provided an important rail and shipping service for area inhabitants. Even prior to the building of the rail link, Kingsport was an important port, though service was sporadic and no scheduled sailings were provided. The rail line brought with it a scheduled shipping connector service commencing in 1893. However, the term "scheduled" may be somewhat misleading since the small ferry *Evangeline* had considerable trouble maintaining the daily crossings of the Minas Basin between Parrsboro and Kingsport, particularly when the weather was unsettled.

DAR NO. 11 ACADIA was most likely at Digby when this undated photo was taken. Its tender is clearly labelled Dominion Atlantic, so it is after 1894. Since it still carries its link and pin coupler, it is before the switch to knuckle couplers in the late 1890s.

The link is the steel bar lying in place down the centre of the pilot. Pins were located on the ends of rolling stock and the links were used to couple the train together. There were inherent dangers in such a system. Not only were there considerable problems in spacing cars to drop the link over the pins, but there were difficulties in getting sufficient slack to allow uncoupling as well. It was no wonder many trainmen of that time lost digits or even limbs. In some cases, trainmen were crushed between cars.

This coupling system had other problems. The pin had oblong holes, which created slack between the cars; there was no standard design for matching links to pins on "foreign" cars; and links were often stolen for their scrap value—all of which caused serious delays. Also the links and pins failed frequently as trains became heavier.

Semi-automatic knuckle couplers were invented in 1868, but the switch to this type of coupler was delayed because they were costly to install. The predecessors of the DAR were disinclined to adopt the new system for financial as well as practical reasons; interchange of cars between the Valley lines would be impossible.

◀ *WCR mystery photo solved, Digby, c. 1890.* PAUL CLEVELAND COLLECTION

⌇ **AS IS OFTEN** the case with historical investigation, there is a great deal of detective work to do, and it sometimes seems as though there are more questions raised with each answer found. As well, new pieces of evidence surface in a random fashion. Although this photograph lacked any inscription, we know that WESTERN No. 3 was delivered to the WCR in 1889, just two years before the Missing Link was completed. Note the gleam on the locomotive's boiler sheeting—evidence of some wiper's pride and effort. Note also the typical WCR finishing touches on the station at right.

The turntable and engine house provided conclusive evidence that the setting is Digby. The presence of the turntable—the large, circular covered structure at the lower right—also narrowed the time frame for the picture. From 1879 to 1891 ferries shuttled passengers and freight around the Missing Link, across the Annapolis Basin, between Digby and Annapolis Royal. After the Dominion government stepped in and completed the Digby–Annapolis Royal segment in 1891, the Digby turntable was no longer essential, and it was moved to a new site on the DAR.

The building of the WCR was difficult to finance adequately, and when the original section extending only from Yarmouth to Digby was put into operation, the revenues from freight and passenger service only marginally exceeded operating costs. This was the most significant reason for the prolonged delay in finishing the Missing Link between Digby and Annapolis.

CHAPTER 2

THE EARLY DAR 1894–1912

FORMATION OF THE DAR

BY 1878 IT WAS APPARENT THAT THE DOMINION AND PROVINCIAL GOVERNMENTS WOULD NEED TO INTERcede to solve the problems plaguing the Valley railways. The obvious solution was to amalgamate the Halifax-to-Yarmouth lines with a single management. One means to accomplish this hinged on the provincial government's original agreements by which they had retained the future right to purchase the lines. In 1880 the provincial government acted on its power to do so by advertising all their lines for sale with the proviso that the sole owner would complete, maintain, and operate them as one railway. Various negotiations took place over the next two years, but without results.

The lack of a serious bidder led the province to enact legislation to consolidate the Nova Scotia Railway (NSR). After consolidation, the Dominion government turned the Windsor Branch over to the province, thus ending their involvement in who would operate the Branch. It was not until 1884 that tentative bids to purchase were tendered. This followed the Dominion's provision of funds to build three large and expensive bridges along the Missing Link. Work on the link progressed steadily but slowly and was completed in 1891.

During that period, the W&AR had been generating such profits that they began serious negotiations to acquire the WCR. In 1893 a group of financiers, including the owners of the W&AR and some WCR investors, agreed to purchase the WCR. Its name was changed briefly to the Yarmouth and Annapolis Railway in 1893 and its sale was approved. Since the W&AR had an agreement with the province to operate the Windsor Branch, the entire Valley line was now under one management group. In July 1894 the Yarmouth and Annapolis Railway, the Windsor and Annapolis Railway, and the Windsor Branch became part of the Dominion Atlantic Railway. The first trains ran on October 1, 1894.

First DAR train, October 1, 1894.

✍ **IT WAS A PROUD** day and the start of what became nearly a century of service by the Dominion Atlantic Railway Company. The first official passenger train eastbound from Yarmouth to Halifax was preparing to leave Yarmouth. DAR No. 18 DIGBY, and the former No. 6 of the Yarmouth and Annapolis Railway (Western Counties Railway), was decorated as befitted the occasion. Besides the various garlands and wreaths, it carried two Union Jacks on either side of the headlight and an inverted horseshoe with a "Good Luck" sign in front of the headlight.

At the same time in Halifax an opposing westbound train, led by DAR No. 16 ATALANTA, was also set to leave.

Although this was the first official day of DAR operations, there was sufficient preparation time before the event to allow DAR lettering to be applied to the tender and a new brass DAR number plate to be fitted to the smoke box door. In fact, it was on July 23, 1894, that the act was passed authorizing the purchase of the Yarmouth and Annapolis Railway by the Windsor and Annapolis Railway and the change of the W&AR's name to the DAR. The actual sale took effect on October 1, 1894. The DAR was incorporated by Parliament on July 22, 1895.

THE MIDLAND RAILWAY

Rail access to the potentially important farmlands and timber and mining resources found in the area between Windsor and Truro was discussed for years. It was the same argument heard about other railways built at that time: travel on rough roads to Windsor or Halifax, or to small ports along the Minas Basin where ships could load, was slow and arduous; a rail line to move goods and people quickly and safely was essential to the development of the area.

In 1896, two years after the formation of the DAR, the Midland Railway Company was formed. Building of the MR, or the Midland as it was known locally, began in 1898 along a direct interior route following the St. Croix and Kennetcook Rivers between Windsor and Truro. It was obvious from the beginning that the line would be a valuable asset to the DAR, and the owners of the DAR began plans to acquire it. Negotiations to buy the Midland began in 1901. To maintain goodwill, and probably as a cost-saving measure, in 1902 the DAR agreed to let the Midland use their Windsor yards and servicing facilities.

Residents along the Cobequid Bay were opposed to the sale. They wanted their own DAR line along the coast. They were appeased by a DAR proposal to build such a line; however, this was never formalized after the agreement to purchase the Midland was signed in 1905.

Midland 4-4-0
No. 3 WINDSOR.
WILLIAM A. STEPHENS /
ANDREA LYNN COLLECTION

↪ **THE MIDLAND RAILWAY** was short-lived. It was bought by the DAR as soon as it was completed in 1905; thus, photographs of rolling stock labelled MIDLAND are rare. When I printed this image from a small collection of glass plate negatives and the letters on Midland No. 3 were visible, its inclusion in the book was a foregone conclusion.

MR No. 3 became DAR No. 29 BROOKLYN in October 1905. A total of four Midland locomotives became part of the DAR. Three of them—Midland Nos. 1, 2, and 3—were renumbered DAR Nos. 31, 30, and 29 and named for communities served by the line (WINDSOR, TRURO, and BROOKLYN). The fourth locomotive,

Midland No. 4, was renumbered No. 28 and named PIONEER. It was the DAR's only 2-6-0 or Mogul type (page 26).

The DAR welcomed construction of the Midland Railway, with the expectation from the outset that they would own it someday. However, the Midland also connected with the ICR in Truro, so the DAR manager was careful to keep favour with the MR owners by allowing the Midland to use DAR facilities.

The Midland remained a very busy subdivision of the DAR for many years, providing a shortcut to the Annapolis Valley that provided cost savings by getting traffic destined to the Valley off the CNR and onto CPR tracks sooner.

Canada No. 27, 1903. BALDWIN LOCOMOTIVE WORKS

The long-standing tradition of taking formally posed builder's shots was carried out with the greatest of care, and the images were always exquisitely sharp. The image in this case is of the newly built DAR No. 27 as it was rolled out of Baldwin Locomotive Works plant in Philadelphia, Pennsylvania, in November 1903. Note that the locomotive is not hot; there is no smoke rising from stack. The locomotive would be moved dead-in-tow (without creating steam) until it reached the DAR. To facilitate this, its drive rods were removed to allow the drive wheels to roll freely and the engine was towed in freight trains using various railways.

No. 27 was built new for the railway as were Nos. 25 and 26, seen on pages 28 and 23. The three were connected in several other ways. Soon after its arrival, the newer No. 27 replaced No. 25 in service on the DAR's accommodation passenger Trains 93 and 94, between Halifax and Yarmouth. Seventeen years later, Nos. 26 and 27 were double-heading a westbound freight just beyond Truro. Unfortunately, there was dense, patchy fog that obscured a cow on the tracks. The engineer braked but the lead locomotive hit the cow and left the track, plowing into the ground; the second locomotive, driven by a second crew, ran into the back of the first locomotive, crushing the cab and killing the fireman. No. 27's frame was twisted in the wreck, and as a result it was scrapped in 1923.

Van hop; No. 26 at Kentville, 1910.

This photo was displayed for years in the Humphrey Club's room at the east end of the Kentville station. As demands for space in the station decreased, the DAR management had donated the room to the retired railwaymen. It was a popular drop-in site for years and was the place where I interviewed a small crowd of members while researching my first book.

The five men posed beside this c. 1910 photograph of DAR 4-4-0 No. 26 PRESIDENT were, from the right, Arthur Hayes, Maurice Williams, Addy Nichols, Ben Yould, and Grover Cleveland. The engine crew is easy to identify by their coveralls, while the conductor and two trainmen are dressed in passenger-service uniforms. The train must have been involved in passenger service, since trainmen only wore their uniforms while working on passenger trains.

The reason the train was running light (without cars), making a caboose hop, is unknown; nobody in the Humphrey Club seemed to know the circumstances, and there is nothing about it recorded on the back of the image.

The van (caboose) was DAR No. 3. The locomotive was DAR No. 26 PRESIDENT, which when built was virtually identical to DAR 4-4-0 No. 25 STRATHCONA (page 28). Even a cursory comparison of the photographs reveals some significant differences. This, of course, was related to mechanical upgrades and changes to paint schemes between 1910 and 1936. At the respective times these two photographs were taken, the 1910 look was very much like the brand new engines would look in 1901. The 1936 image shows how the engines would have appeared c. 1941, when both of these engines were scrapped.

Bear River bridge, c. 1912. GARY NESS COLLECTION

There have been two 1,700-foot railway bridges across the Bear River. The work on the first one, shown in this photograph, was done by Dominion government contractors in 1889 and 1890. Soon after, on August 21, 1890, the first train, an ICR work train, ran from Yarmouth to Digby across the Missing Link.

This photo reveals interesting features of the bridge, including the turntable section under the last car of the train. The square, wood-sheathed ends of the piers are visible, as are the wooden supports of the spans.

The high-tide marks are readily apparent on the piers, which were too low, exposing wood bridge components to damage. The tides in this estuary, which ranged up to thirty feet, were affected by prevailing winds from the north. These drove more water into the river mouth on many occasions. Additionally, ice chunks created in winter pounded away at the wood coverings of the square-ended foundations, and in some extreme weather, at the bridge supports themselves.

Construction of a replacement bridge began in 1912. It was built fifty feet downstream and ran parallel to the first. It faced exactly the same construction challenges as the first and one more, which was related to the proximity of the first bridge's foundation piers to the caissons of the new bridge's piers. Tidal flows peaked at four miles per hour and involved massive water movements, creating eddies that would undermine the supports for the first bridge; however, it had to serve until the new one was operational. To prevent such problems the old bridge was shored extensively so that damage to a pier would not result in collapse.

CHAPTER 3

THE DAR/CPR ERA: THE EARLY YEARS 1912–1940

Mogul DAR No. 28 PIONEER, Windsor, 1914.
GARY NESS COLLECTION

IT WAS QUITE EXCITING TO FIND THIS PRINT OF LOCO-MOTIVE NO. 28 PIONEER, THE ONLY 2-6-0 OR MOGUL TYPE on the DAR. Pictures of it are quite rare; I have seen only two others, and they do not show the locomotive well. This one does, but unfortunately it has not aged well. The original print was faded noticeably and turned a brownish shade due to incomplete washing when it was made (a lot of old photographs are lost due to this effect). To make matters much worse, something was spilled on the print and a wrinkled plastic cover was attached over the emulsion. Although the photograph was a mess, it had to be included because of its historical merits. It has been restored electronically as much as possible.

The train was at Windsor on August 10, 1914. The train's crew included conductor C. Pentz (at right), engineer Bill Young (second from right), and trainmen Clarke Barnaby, Ben Greenough, Bill Hopkins, and E. Crosby, all clustered near and on the front end.

DAR No. 28 was built in 1904 as the Midland Railway No. 4, one year before the DAR purchased the Midland. Although it was an unusual type, the DAR must have viewed it as somewhat successful because it lasted as long as its three Midland mates, which were scrapped c. 1920.

World War One troop train, parlour car ANNAPOLIS ROYAL on the end, Wolfville, 1915.
A. L. HARDY / GARY NESS COLLECTION

It was June 18, 1915, when the DAR's official photographer recorded this image at the Wolfville station. No other details were recorded, but it would appear that this Halifax-bound train was carrying troops, probably from Aldershot Military Camp, which was established by the British in the 1890s as a training area for Nova Scotia militia units. Canada's Department of Militia and Defence took it over in 1906. It was expanded somewhat during World War One. Troops were housed in tents but permanent cookhouses, messes, and a camp hospital were built. Over seven thousand troops were trained there during World War One.

The men on the station platform in this scene are unidentified, but they clearly were high-ranking officers who were deliberately posed.

The DAR's actions in World War One involved more than just troop movements. Because DAR General Manager George Graham was parked at the North Street station when the 1917 Halifax explosion occurred, a DAR relief train was one of the first to arrive in Halifax.

Later, the *Halifax Herald* chartered a special DAR train—at the considerable sum of two thousand dollars—to race to the Valley carrying free copies of the paper, which announced the end of World War One. The paper also kept the telegraph lines busy disseminating the message.

This marvellous photograph shows DAR No. 25 STRATHCONA with Train 95. The summer 1915 public timetable indicated two westbound trains between Yarmouth and Halifax, the Mail Express Train 95, which was the regular, year-round fast passenger train, and the Flying Bluenose Train 123, the summer-only train. Both trains ran daily except for Sundays. The typical consist for the Flying Bluenose had a buffet-parlour car on the tail end and salon coaches ahead of that car. From the pattern of windows along the sides of the last car, that one appears to be a standard coach, and this train must be Train 95.

The Flying Bluenose met the ferry owned by the Boston and Yarmouth Steamship Company Ltd. and embarked passengers who had made the seventeen-hour overnight trip from Boston. The train left Yarmouth at 9:10 AM, arriving at Kentville at 1:58 PM and Halifax at 4:40 PM. There were few stops along the way for this train: Weymouth, Digby, Annapolis, Bridgetown, Middleton, Kentville, Wolfville, Windsor, and Windsor Junction. Train 95 made the same stops, but the stop in Digby was extended in order to meet the Saint John ferry. The Flying Bluenose and the Mail Express left Yarmouth twenty minutes apart, at 9:10 AM and 9:30 AM respectively, but arrived at Halifax at 4:40 PM and 6:45 PM.

DAR Boarding Car 851 with a monitor roof, Kentville, post 1915.
GARY NESS COLLECTION

It was difficult to learn much about this image of former W&AR first-class coach No. 6 GRACIOSA, built in 1869.

Doug Phillips noted there is a possibility it was acquired "new" by the W&AR; the records he found at CP indicated it was built by W&AR. In other research about CPR cars, however, he found that CPR's records showed the car builder as the railway it was acquired from, which was sometimes incorrect. Phillips also noted it may have been CPR's way of recording the car's history if the builder was not recorded by the previous road.

Obviously, the GRACIOSA served on both the W&AR and the DAR. Although we do know that it was renumbered by the DAR as 851 and served as a boarding car after 1915, little else has been discovered. It was scrapped in 1939.

The car was quite distinctive with the monitor roof, an early version of the clerestory type. The monitor roof was already becoming obsolete around the time this car was built by the W&AR.

There are other photos of it in the Merrilees Transportation Collection at the Library and Archives Canada. One of those images shows the car with an oblong board beneath the windows on the side of the coach. One might surmise that this was its nameplate during its service as a passenger coach.

That same collection has images of similar combine and baggage cars; none show a monitor roof. There appears to be very little information about those images also.

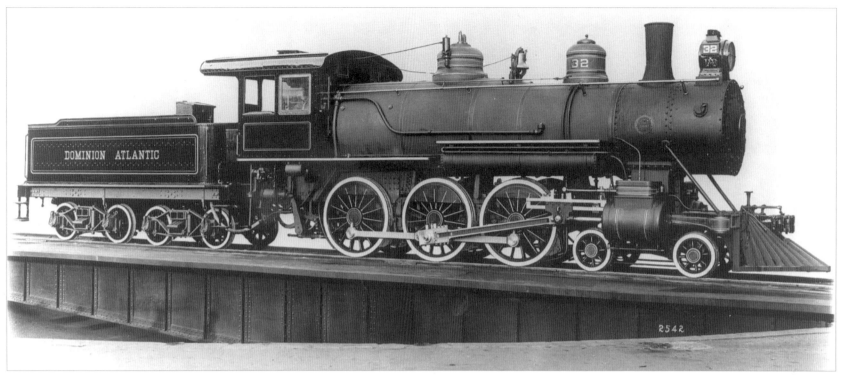

DAR No. 32, Philadelphia, PA, 1907. BALDWIN LOCOMOTIVE WORKS / AL PATERSON COLLECTION

Here, No. 32 BLOMIDON appears in a Baldwin Locomotive Works builder's photograph at Philadelphia, Pennsylvania, in October 1907 and on the next page in the late 1930s at Kentville, a few years prior to scrapping. It was one of the small group of six locomotives built for the DAR that was present on the line when the CPR purchased it in 1912. This locomotive and an identical copy, No. 33 GLOOSCAP, were the last two locomotives built by the DAR; all locomotives (but one) used subsequently on the line were standard CPR types.

Close inspection of the photos reveals some interesting changes in the locomotive's external appearance over time. Some of the changes were more obvious than others.

Although the photographs could only have been in black and white, we know that the colour schemes changed. There is ample proof to conclude that in the 1907 photo, No. 32 was painted magenta and black and striped so that the DAR need only apply finishing touches. Careful inspection of the locomotive image reveals fine double gold stripes around the domes, gold numbers on the sand dome, the DAR script logo on the sides of the headlight just below the number thirty-two and headlight, double gold striping on the piston and piston head, and the rectangular double stripe under the window on the cab side panel, which would bear the name BLOMIDON after final details *(CONTINUED NEXT PAGE)*

No. 32 on Kentville turntable, 1930s.
EDGAR DEWOLFE

were completed by the DAR. The tender bears a rectangle of double, fine gold stripes framing the railway name, which at this time was applied in a straight line. The paint scheme, striping, and identification of the engine underwent several significant changes during the locomotive's years of service.

For example, in both photos, the smoke box front is black, in contrast to the view of No. 32 that appears on page 38 in which the smoke box is silver or white. This was done for a very short time, from 1938 until 1942. Apparently it improved visibility of the oncoming train, but also was viewed by employees and observers alike as an aesthetic improvement. This information would indicate that the above photo of No. 32 at Kentville was taken prior to 1938.

There also were numerous changes to No. 32's mechanical features. In the 1930s image, there is a shorter smoke box with a different access door on the front, and the boiler has been stepped down in diameter at the junction between the boiler jacket and the smoke box. There is a shade above the engineer's side window and a foldaway windscreen is attached to the front edge of his window. The headlight was swapped and marker lights were added at base of the stack. A CPR standard small tender, with an upward extension of the coal bunker, had replaced the original builder's version.

No. 556, the Digby switcher.
A. H. COVERDALE
COLLECTION

This image depicts No. 556 working as the Digby switcher. Notice the footboard (step) that has replaced the usual cowcatcher (pilot).

There were three tracks on the wharf, two of which were on the northern side of the freight shed (page 70). Two express cars would already be positioned on one of the tracks when the fast passenger trains arrived. Both cars were added to the eastbound train. One express car was destined for Halifax; the other would be set off at Windsor and taken on to Truro later that day on Train 7, the Windsor-Truro Mixed.

Another 500 class locomotive (No. 504) had brought a typical six-car consist comprising a baggage, mail, and express cars, two coaches and a parlour car to Digby. The front end of the train, the baggage, mail, and express cars would be backed onto the wharf by No. 504. The Digby switcher, usually a 500 class 4-6-0 like No. 556, would couple to the two coaches and parlour car and back these onto the wharf. Passengers would then be transferred and this portion of the train would be returned to the main line in front of the station. The head end, drawn by No. 504, would set off the express car for return to Yarmouth on Train 95, pick up the two express cars for Halifax and Truro, and reattach to the waiting coaches and parlour car in front of the station. The train would then depart for Halifax.

Spring floods, Kentville, 1920. GARY NESS COLLECTION

Spring floods of the railway associated with snowmelt and rain were common in many places but had an added complication when tidal influences were also at work. The Cornwallis River, like all upper Bay of Fundy rivers, experienced twice-daily tides, which could vary in depth from thirty-six to forty-nine feet. These tidal waters migrated inland for long distances, and in the case of the Cornwallis River, as far as Kentville. This back flow of water temporarily holds back the spring runoff; the flood water piles up and then rushes to the sea with considerable force as the tide recedes. This March 14, 1920 photograph, shows "the Flat" on the north side of the Kentville DAR yard. Railway workers knew from experience that this bridge could be swept away and to lessen that possibility used locomotives like No. 29 ANNAPOLIS to add weight during the spring runoff.

Over the years reports of such floods were numerous. For example, on April 1, 1904, the DAR was at a standstill with washouts from rain and fast spring melts. The worst-hit areas were the Lawrencetown-Bridgetown and Port Williams–Kentville sections. In some places the water rose between two and four feet over the rails, created gullies in the roadbed, caused erosion around trestles, and left behind large quantities of troublesome drift-ice chunks. The spring of 1936 was another disastrous year, when an abnormally fast spring thaw and heavy rains flooded many sections of the railway. On March 13, 1936, the entire DAR was closed for twenty-four hours. The Kentville–Yarmouth and the Midlands sections were closed for forty-eight hours with trains stranded at various places by the floods and drift ice on the railway. The Weston Branch would remain closed until the end of March.

DAR No. 36, Windsor, 1921. HAROLD A. JENKINS / GARY NESS COLLECTION

DAR No. 36 BASIL was CPR No. 320 prior to its sale to the DAR in October 1911. It was one of three CPR small 4-6-0s sold to the DAR just before the CPR lease took effect.

The two other CPR locomotives included in that sale, Nos. 310 and 319, became DAR No. 34 GASPEREAUX and No. 35 GABRIEL. These small 4-6-0 types did not last long once the CPR took over. The CPR almost immediately implemented a plan to upgrade the DAR to CPR standards, which required heavier locomotives based on its traffic, such as the CPR D6 4-6-0 type with numbers in the 500s. The retirement of the old, smaller locomotives began in earnest in 1917. CPR records show that BASIL was the first ex-CPR

4-6-0 to be scrapped—in June 1917. GABRIEL and GAPEREAUX lasted six more years and were scrapped in 1923.

This photograph of No. 36 BASIL in the Windsor yard is dated 1921, a date that may be a mistake given that CPR records show it was scrapped in 1917. However, Harold Jenkins, a notable DAR photographer, also was known for his careful record keeping, so one wonders.

Interestingly, some of the dwellings in this scene are still present today; however, Highway 101 now crosses the area between the railway and the homes.

The known roster of 0-6-0 types on the DAR includes two engines that were sold to the line. These were both former CPR engines, U3c No. 6189 and U3d No. 6227 (page 71). They arrived in 1937 and 1939, respectively. No. 6189 was scrapped in 1939, while No. 6227 was scrapped much later in 1957. There is photographic evidence that at least three other 0-6-0s were loaned or leased to the DAR; these included CPR U2f No. 6058, U3c No. 6161, and CPR U3a No. 0-6-0 6109, shown here.

Interestingly, this photo may be a previously unknown photograph of a locomotive that was loaned or leased temporarily to the DAR, and while on the line it was identified as a DAR locomotive.

There appears to be a very faded "Land of Evangeline" herald on its tender. This was not supposed to happen. The apparent fading of the herald suggests that the locomotive either was on the DAR for a long time or there was a lot of dirt on the side panel of the tender. Thin gold striping on the tender side panel was also visible but faded.

There was no information with the negative. All that can be deduced from the image with any certainty is that it was taken on the turntable in Kentville. We do know that No. 6109 was sold to the Dominion Steel and Coal Corporation in 1934, so the date for this photograph must be prior to that.

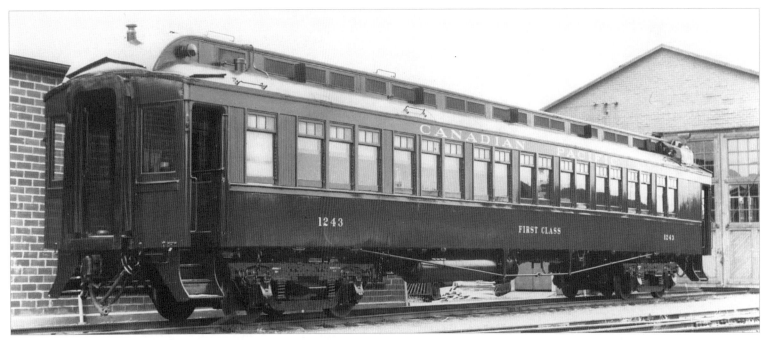

DAR first-class coach No. 1243.

HAROLD A. JENKINS / GARY NESS COLLECTION

CPR Coach No. 691 was built in 1903 at their Hochelaga shops; it was renumbered to CPR No. 1243 in 1912 as a first-class and smoking coach with sixty-four seats. It was converted to work service in 1949, renumbered CPR No. 411517, and scrapped in 1960 at west Toronto.

Although it is conjecture, it is easy to conclude that the CPR had loaned, rather than sold, the No. 1243 coach to the DAR to meet the need for more passenger coaches and that it was returned to CPR later. To the best of my knowledge, there is no record of this CPR coach on the DAR except this photo. Also if the recorded assignment of locomotives was any indication, rolling stock transfers to affiliates would have been recorded by CPR only if sold. Temporary loans were not logged, and loaned items were not supposed to be relabelled as DAR. It seems reasonable to conjecture that the same

practice applied to this coach; certainly the timing is correct given the date—1935. Also, the later renumbering into the CP system indicated a return transfer back to the CPR.

In 1935, when the photo of FIRST CLASS Coach No. 1243 was taken, DAR patrons considered the coach the ideal way to travel. In an earlier era, the DAR had discovered that labelling the best coaches first class to distinguish them from other coaches resulted in other coaches having fewer passengers. The solution from a business point of view was obvious—to upgrade that part of the fleet with a coat of paint, somewhat better seating, and application of the label *first class*. Apparently, this ensured usage. These aging wooden coaches would not have qualified as first class elsewhere on the CPR, which was by this time replacing these old cars with "modern" steel coaches.

No. 26 KENT,
Kentville,
1936.
HAROLD A.
JENKINS / GARY
NESS COLLECTION

It was near the end for the 4-4-0 types on the DAR. Many of them had been retired and scrapped in the 1920s. Nos. 23 and 24 lasted until 1939 and Nos. 25 and 26 lasted only slightly longer. DAR trains had become far too heavy for these diminutive locomotives to handle alone. Even the heavier 500 class 4-6-0s were not sufficient to the task; thus, double-heading had become too regular an occurrence. This was a very expensive operating practice since such trains required two locomotives and two locomotive crews.

This perfectly lit three-quarter roster shot of KENT recorded one of four of the DAR's 4-4-0s in the last paint scheme these would receive. Within a year, the CPR would begin sending much larger D10 4-6-0s and G2 4-6-2s to the line. The small locos would be scrapped, the last of them going in 1941. Although nobody could know it, the use of brass nameplates was near an end, too; the World War Two effort would need brass for shell casings.

The locomotive spent its final years switching the Kentville yard, hauling the school trains, Trains 12 inbound to Kentville and 13 outbound to Kingsport, as well as Trains 11 to Kingsport and 14 returning to Kentville on the Cornwallis Branch line. These trains intersected with the MV *Kipawo* ferry service in those years.

No. 32 at
Kentville,
late 1930s,
cinders train.
JAMES WALDER
COLLECTION

This photograph, taken from a flatcar on an adjacent track, shows Ten-wheeler No. 32 BLOMIDON, powering a work train in Kentville during the locomotive's final months, sometime between September 1938 (the inspection date stencilled on the flatcar side) and 1941 when the locomotive was scrapped. The absence of leaves on the deciduous bushes, the winterization curtains hanging at the rear of BLOMIDON's cab, and the appearance of the new stencil on the flatcar all suggest that this was probably taken during the early winter of 1938.

Pride in the DAR's locomotive fleet is demonstrated by a number of interesting features revealed in this photograph. The paint scheme applied to the locomotive is characteristic of the time. The boiler, cylinders, cab sides, drivers, and tender were painted Tuscan red. Gold striping in a rectangular pattern was applied to frame the tender side panels, and although it is not clearly visible, the elaborate "Land of Evangeline" herald graces the tender side panels. All wheel rims, plus the walkway edges and the smoke box front, were painted white while the rest of the locomotive was black. Even though this locomotive is depicted in work train service, note the sheen of its boiler sheathing. The highly detailed cast brass number plate adorning the smoke box door and the brass nameplate serve as finishing touches.

Ski train, Ellershouse, 1936. J. C. M. HAYWARD / PAUL CLEVELAND COLLECTION

There were some interesting puzzles associated with this photograph. The caption noted on the back of it suggests that the occasion involved the "first ski train" at Ellershouse on February 23, 1936. Retired DAR trainmen and operators did not recall any special ski trains and very little was discovered about the scene until a newspaper article, dated February 17, 1936, was found by Carl Riff. It remarked that between fifty and one hundred skiers and outdoor enthusiasts were ready to ride the first-ever DAR ski train special from Halifax to Ellershouse. Apparently, the response was so enthusiastic it was suggested that more such specials might occur during the winter. It is unknown if this happened.

The train was an extra or unscheduled run, as indicated by the white flags displayed on either side of the locomotive's headlight. Some of the seven men posing in the foreground have been identified: engineer Arthur (Jigs) Ells is at the far right, trainman John Lightle is in the middle, and conductor Ernie Hartlen is third from the left.

Ellershouse was located at Mile 23.3 of the Halifax Subdivision, the former Windsor Branch of the NSR. Photographs of trains on this section of the DAR—the oldest segment of the railway—are rare.

No. 500 does not yet bear its nameplate (MEMBERTOU) because it was still on loan and would not be sold to the DAR until 1937.

This stunning wide-angle photograph was commissioned by R. A. Jodrey during the mid-1930s, presumably to document the pulpwood operations at the Hantsport headquarters of Jodrey's growing business empire.

The photographer (Harold A. Jenkins?) made the original negative, approximately thirty-six inches long, with a circuit camera. The negative was held in a typical film holder at the rear of the bellows camera, which had an unusual lens. The lens had to be of excellent optical quality to produce the side-to-side sharpness apparent here. The lens functioned by rotating a thin vertical line of light across the film at the correct speed to expose the film properly. The negative was already very large so use of a print enlarger was not

necessary. Instead the negative was sandwiched with glass on top of a piece of photographic paper, and a timed exposure to light created contact prints that were exactly the same size as the negative.

The scene has many points of interest. The transport cargo steamship SS *Dago*, at the dock, was built in 1902 by the Caledon Shipbuilding & Engineering Company Ltd., Dundee, and was owned by the Ellerman Wilson Line; it sailed with a British registry. Men who worked in Hantsport remembered seeing the vessel tied up there frequently. The ship was sunk in World War Two during a 1942 air raid off Portugal while en route to Oporto from Lisbon.

In this photo the piles of pulpwood on the dock are being loaded into the hold. Tales about this process *(CONTINUED NEXT PAGE)*

reveal that it was hard work, with some parts of the job preferable based on the time of year. The bales of pulpwood were often still hot from processing, and seasoned longshoremen would send their less knowledgeable, usually younger co-workers to work in the hold during the summer and onto the docks during the winter. The hold was very hot in the summer months but quite pleasant in the winter months.

DAR crews recount their own tales about the site. While it is not visible, the siding behind the train led onto the dock, where a facing switch track alignment—due to lack of space for a normal siding—often required jigging or a flying switch to position cars on the dock. The crew would back this train, with the car behind the engine No. 556 to the end of the reversing track, and then accelerate forward to give the car just enough momentum to move on its own. They would then uncouple the car from the locomotive on the fly, accelerate the locomotive over the reversing switch to clear it, then throw the switch to divert the car along the track leading onto the dock. A trainman riding on the car would use the handbrake on the car to stop it in the correct place. Obviously failure to get the right speed and time for routing both the locomotive and freight car could be problematic. Nonetheless, crews did it successfully all the time because the alternative was a very time-consuming, inefficient operation.

Train connections to ferries and ships that offered transport between ports on the Minas Basin dated back to 1858 and the completion of the Windsor Branch. Prior to the building of the western extensions through the Annapolis Valley, access to those ships offered a considerable time-saving and cost-cutting service for transporting people and goods to the areas bounded by the Minas Basin and the Bay of Fundy.

The SS *Evangeline*, a small sloop built in 1882 at Hantsport, could handle twenty-five tons of cargo but had a small 50hp steam engine, which meant that its top speed was less than 10 knots. This steamship was first associated with railway operations in 1884 when it acted as the ferry between Annapolis Royal and Digby during the years of the Missing Link on the WCR. When that rail line was completed in 1891, the ship was purchased by the fledgling W&AR, which created the Evangeline Navigation Company to run their own Minas Basin ferry service between Kingsport and Parrsboro.

When the DAR was formed in 1894, it also acquired the ferry service. The *Evangeline* continued in   *(CONTINUED NEXT PAGE)*

The MV Kipawo, Wolfville, late 1930s.
EDGAR DEWOLFE

service until 1904, when the DAR needed a new, larger vessel, and the SS *Prince Albert* was bought. Although the fifty-ton steamer capable of speed up to 12 knots was larger, it too was a small coastal steamer. It serviced the two previous ports of call, as well as a third, Wolfville, but like the *Evangeline*, it struggled to maintain a schedule whenever weather and tides opposed it.

The *Prince Albert* was replaced in 1926 because it was underpowered, and perhaps more importantly a ship was needed that could carry cars. The service was upgraded substantially with the purchase of the MV *Kipawo*, which had been built in Saint John a year earlier. Along with the larger, more powerful ferry, the DAR upgraded the service by installing waiting rooms along with freight sheds at each terminal; the shed at the right was the waiting area for ferry- or train-bound passengers.

The photograph at the left shows the *Kipawo* entering Wolfville's harbour on the high tide after crossing the Minas Basin from Kingsport. The ferry's railway crest on the bow is very prominent. The ship was readily capable of maintaining a sailing schedule, but the vagaries of the tide and the shallow harbours at the three ports caused the railway to have unscheduled meets with the trains.

The ship could carry just over 120 passengers and up to 8 cars; the photograph on this page shows the crew doing just that. A car was in the cradle that was designed for this task and could be hoisted in the air and swung on or off the ship on the pivoting boom.

The Minas Basin ferry service ended during World War Two, when the *Kipawo* and Captain Trefry were needed for anti-submarine service off Newfoundland. They left in April 1941.

DAR employee picnic, Grand-Pré, late 1930s.
EDGAR DEWOLFE

According to J. B. King, "excursions ran thither and yon" in the early days. In fact, DAR excursions continued to run for many years. Excursions were sometimes revenue generating but goodwill was often a reason. For example, this c. 1939 train was a DAR employee's family picnic at Grand-Pré Park. The train ran return from Kentville to Grand-Pré, with a long stop for the picnic.

The train consist was quite deliberate with two locomotives placed back to back to have a leading locomotive with its pilot truck facing in the direction of travel. To keep this alignment, the locomotives switched ends on the train while the picnic occurred. The pilot truck on steam engines served to guide the drive wheels into curves when running at speed. Smaller diameter wheels followed the curving track alignment better than the large diameter drivers, which sometimes tended to roll up and over a curving rail.

The baggage car was deliberately behind the locomotive tender to act as a "buffer car" between the steel tender and the wooden passenger cars. The buffer car was standard safety practice to prevent "telescoping" in a head-on collision, in which the wood car behind the tender would jam forward around the steel tender much the way telescope pieces slide together. Clearly, this would be disastrous for passengers in wooden cars. The advent of more modern steel passenger cars prevented such occurrences; however, due to cost, many secondary lines continued to use wooden cars for many years after the main line trains had switched to steel cars.

Double-headed gypsum train, Wolfville, late 1930s.
EDGAR DEWOLFE

Prior to the development of a docking facility for deepwater, ocean-going vessels at Hantsport in 1947, gypsum was loaded on smaller ships at two sites. In the summer, ships were loaded from the dock at the Wentworth plant at Dimock's. Winter ice prevented use of this shallow estuary, and gypsum was transferred by rail from Dimock's and stockpiled at Deep Brook on the Annapolis Basin, just west of Annapolis Royal. While the modern facility at Hantsport allowed for a year-round loading of much larger ships, it did not resolve all the tidal problems inherent near the head of the Bay of Fundy. This body of water rises and falls thirty-five feet twice daily, which leaves the Hantsport dock dry at low tide. Large ships could not rest on the bottom without risk of breaking in two; thus, they arrived, loaded,

and departed within a three-hour period available at high tide.

These locomotives would be making light work of this east-bound train of empty gypsum hoppers at Wolfville in the late 1930s. The train was an extra, indicated by the white flags to either side of No. 2511's stack. Gypsum trains required double-heading, a practice that was a problem at the Clementsport bridge because it had weight restrictions. The solution was to get the train moving westbound from Annapolis Royal using two locomotives and to then cut off the lead unit on the fly. This engine hurried ahead, crossing the bridge first. The second engine could keep the train moving; the first engine was recoupled on the far side.

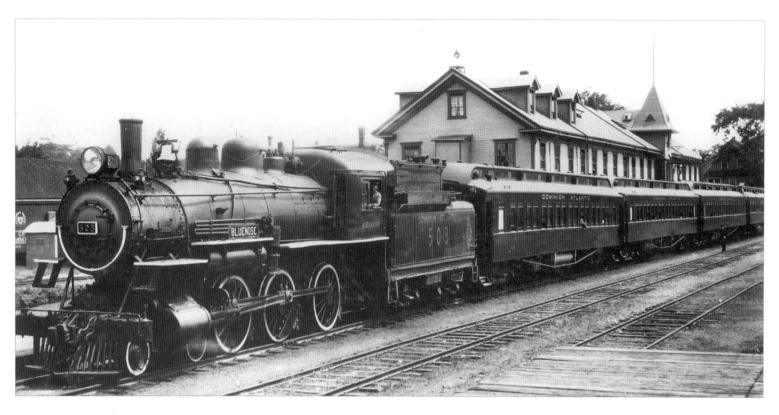

The Flying Bluenose.

At first glance, the photographs on these adjoining pages appear to be very similar; however, close inspection reveals many differences between the two images.

Here, the locomotive and crew change have been completed and the DAR's famous summer tourist train, the Flying Bluenose Train 123, was ready for its westbound departure from Kentville at 1:45 PM. Stops for this fastest of all DAR passenger trains included Windsor Junction, Windsor, Wolfville, Kentville, Middleton, Annapolis Royal, Digby (where the train met the Saint John ferry), Weymouth, Meteghan, and Yarmouth. Stops were very brief, except at Kentville and Digby, and even then early timetables reveal that a typical stop for the Flying Bluenose at Kentville lasted only ten minutes. In Digby, a similar ten-minute schedule was allowed for the meet with the ferry to Saint John, New Brunswick. Later timetables show somewhat longer stops, but these were still brief, limited to less than twenty-five minutes.

In the summer of 1886 the W&AR commenced operation of the train, which bore two names temporarily—the Flying Bluenose on the eastbound runs and the Flying Acadian on the westbound trips. It ran four times per week on schedules that were much faster than the regular express trains of the day. The W&AR dropped the Flying Acadian label for the westbound train, calling both operations the Flying Bluenose when the train recommenced summer service on August 4, 1891, just after the Missing Link was completed and run-through operation from Halifax to Yarmouth began.

The New Yorker,
c. 1940.

No. 502 had been added to Train 25R, the New Yorker, and the engineer and conductor were photographed during the obligatory check of watches prior to departure from Kentville. The New Yorker—like the Flying Bluenose—was a summer only special tourist train designed to attract patrons from the lucrative New England market. DAR brochures and public timetables of the pre-World War Two era extolled the virtues of the "Land of Evangeline Route" and the "premier day train service" on their named trains.

No. 502 was labelled in a unique fashion: the lettering on the tender led to one suggestion, that No. 502 was named the New Yorker. This is highly unlikely; DAR engine names were chosen for their local geographical significance or for their importance as local historical figures. Also, locomotive names were painted on the cab sides (page 46) or later were displayed on brass nameplates mounted on the running boards (page 52). The label on the tender here was undoubtedly the train's name and No. 502 was dedicated to service on the New Yorker for that summer. The date of this photograph was not recorded, but there are a number of details that suggest the date was sometime in 1940, probably just after No. 502 was restored to its original CPR number—it had been DAR No. 44 for a time.

The locomotive would have been a stunning magenta and the boiler, pistons, and unusual apron extending between the smoke box and the pilot were gleaming.

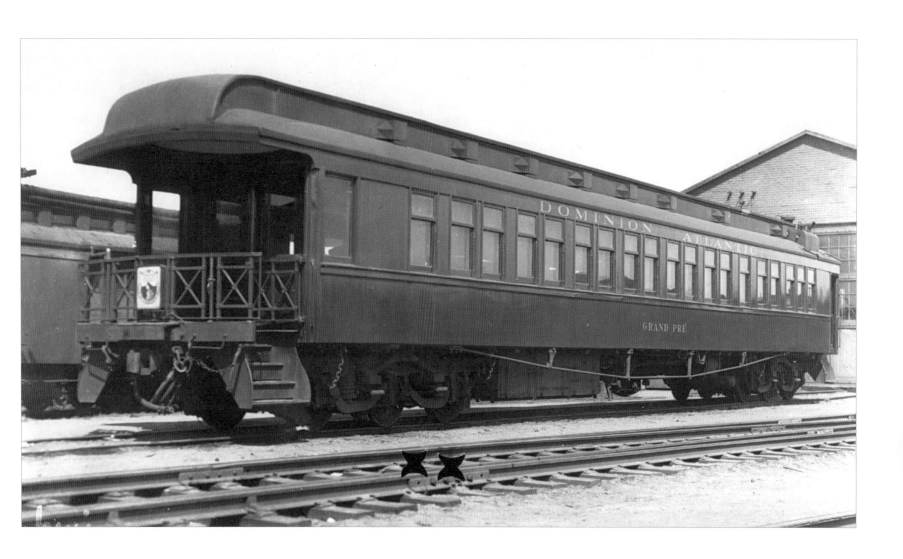

◀ Parlour cars for the Flying Bluenose, 1938. HAROLD A. JENKINS

GRAND PRE, one of the famed DAR buffet-parlour cars, was occupying a Kentville car-shop track in this 1938 scene.

In June 1924 newspaper articles in the *Halifax Herald* extolled the virtues of the DAR's plan to add two new "splendidly appointed" parlour-buffet-observation cars, GRAND PRE and ANNAPOLIS ROYAL. These were luxury upgrades to the Flying Bluenose trains and were intended to build on the DAR successes with the summer tourist traffic. The cars were said to be "the last word" in modern train service.

The articles described the car interiors in detail. Seating was movable chairs covered in a green plush. Axminster's famed carpeting was used throughout in a shade that "corresponded" with the chair colour. The interior woodwork featured mahogany and satinwood, finished to give the cars an "appearance of rare richness."

To get a sense of what the Axminster label meant to people of that era, Axminster Carpets Limited, of Axminster, Devon, England, produced their first carpets in 1755 and are still in business today. Their carpets have been described historically as "the benchmark for wealthy aristocrats to have in their country homes and town houses, between 1755 and 1835."

The patron's experience (page 68) with these DAR cars was felt to be so important that when choking dust from new ballast became a nuisance on the rear platform of the cars in 1937, the DAR went to great efforts with dust abatement equipment and chemicals.

CHAPTER 4

THE DAR/CPR ERA 1940–1956

The "Five-Locomotive Lineup," Kentville, 1937. HAROLD A JENKINS / GARY NESS COLLECTION

THESE PHOTOGRAPHS OF WHAT WAS SOMETIMES RE-FERRED TO AS THE "FIVE LOCOMOTIVE LINEUP" WERE taken in the Kentville yard in May 1937. It is thought the DAR commissioned these publicity shots to mark the arrival of larger CPR steam locomotives on the railway. In addition to showing the different types of locomotives in service on the railway at the time, the photographs provide an interesting contrast between the three smaller locomotives at the right, and which had served the DAR faithfully for many years, and the two new, larger locomotives on the left, which along with others of their type, were about to become the backbone of heavy service on the DAR for the next two decades.

The five locomotives included, from the right, 4-4-0 No. 25 STRATHCONA (later renamed PONTGRAVE for a short time); 4-6-0 No. 32 BLOMIDON; *(CONTINUED NEXT PAGE)*

The "Five-Locomotive Lineup," Kentville, 1937. HAROLD A JENKINS / GARY NESS COLLECTION

4-6-0 No. 544 HEBERT; 4-6-0 No. 999; and 4-6-2 No. 2552. CPR records revealed that No. 544 was sold to the DAR in May 1937, but it is unlikely that it had arrived then. Omer Lavallée has pointed out that CPR engines were loaned or leased to the DAR and could be present for extended periods that company records did not include.

Only sales were recorded officially. Further, No. 544 appears to have a nameplate, while the other new arrivals have not yet had their brass nameplates affixed on the running board. Soon after this photograph was taken, Nos. 999 and 2552 would be fitted with their nameplates, FRONSAC and HALIBURTON, respectively.

Modernization of locomotives.
HAROLD K. VOLLRATH COLLECTION

This was first No. 44 POUTRINCOURT at Kentville during the years 1928–1940. It was originally CPR No. 502 and would be again after 1940.

A lot of early locomotives, including the CPR class D6 Ten-wheelers, were built originally as "compound types" in 1903–1904. Compound engines were popular in the late 1800s and used steam twice, once in two high-pressure pistons and again in two low-pressure pistons. This was thought to be the most cost-efficient use of steam; however, maintaining this equipment was very costly and when boiler superheaters (page x) were developed, the conversion of older CPR engines to superheated, single-steam expansion locomotives followed.

Superheaters provided considerable savings in fuel consumption.

A superheater consisted of long pipes or superheater elements running inside the boiler flues, which were filled with intensely hot gases from the fire. Heat transfer to the steam already created in the boiler reheated the steam in the elements, raising the temperature to the point where steam became dry steam, that is, it was so hot it could not condense back to water. This steam was then passed to the cylinders to drive the side-rods and thus turned the wheels.

For the CPR, these modifications involved removal of the original cylinders, replacement with piston valve cylinders, and modifications to the Stephenson valve gear. Installation of the superheater required significant remodelling of the boiler to install the new flues and the superheater components.

DAR second No. 44 was at Kentville in this 1943 view, the year in which it was sold to the DAR. This was a former Quebec Central Railway (QCR) locomotive of the same number. Examination of the two photos of No. 44 reveal differences between the CPR D6a 4-6-0 and QCR 4-6-0 types, the most obvious of which were the headlights and number boards, the front steps to the footboard/ walkway, the air tanks under the footboard (resulting in a different footboard alignment), the different inward tilt to the pistons, the cab windows, and the tenders, to name only a few.

The first DAR No. 44 POUTRINCOURT was CPR D6a 4-6-0 No. 502 before being sold to the DAR. It was later sold back to the CPR and renumbered CPR No. 502. DAR second No. 44 was built

for the Quebec Central to their own specifications, much like the DAR had designed and built 4-6-0s Nos. 32 and 33. It remains a mystery as to why No. 502 was sold back to the CPR and why the DAR would buy a one-of-a-kind locomotive that required special parts. The CPR D6a, b, c, and d 4-6-0s types were similar enough that one set of parts and tools could be used on all of them.

No. 44 is on the track leading to the roundhouse. It appears that it has just come in from a run and is having its ashpan cleaned. Its coal bunker also appears to be low on coal, so it would take on water, coal, and sand before easing into a roundhouse stall for maintenance.

World War Two was under way when this photograph was taken of double-headed eastbound daily Train M-100 as it pulled away from Yarmouth (*M* identified a mixed freight and passenger train).

Prior to World War Two, frequent double-headers caused the CPR to begin replacing the small 500 class Ten-wheelers; they, like No. 44, were too light to pull the increasingly heavy trains in the 1930s, and double-heading became too common at that time. The practice was expensive because two locomotives and crews were required. The availability of the heavier D10 and G2 classes of locomotives was supposed to greatly diminish double-heading on the DAR; however, the onset of World War Two brought it back.

Every part of the CPR was strained by the war effort, but the DAR much more so due its position in Nova Scotia, where the numerous military bases and the unending movement of war materials resulted in the greatest tonnage ever experienced before or since. In 1940 only six D10s and three G2s were on the DAR, and the sale of more D10s and G2s to the line would not happen again until 1949, well after the exigencies of war eased.

Ten-wheeler No 44 was one of the DAR's oddball locomotives, a former Quebec Central locomotive that somehow was sold the DAR in 1943 and thus managed to remain until it was scrapped in 1954. It was the only example of the type on the DAR.

CPR D10s sold to the DAR; No. 999 at Kentville, 1942.

The CPR D10 4-6-0s were the most numerous steam locomotive type found on any railway in Canada, with over five hundred engines in the class. They were extremely versatile, and as a result they made their way into every corner of the CPR system, including subsidiaries such as the DAR. The initial arrival of the D10 type on the DAR in 1937 was marked by some fanfare. By 1940 many of the smaller steam locomotives were gone, and the D10 Ten-wheelers and G2 Pacifics were the dominant power until the end of steam.

On June 8, 1942, No. 999, a D10h, was seen coupled to hopper cars loaded with ashes and cinders, sitting on the shop tracks in Kentville. No. 999 was among the first four D10s placed in service on the DAR. It arrived in May 1937 and was named FRONSAC. Three other D10h locomotives arrived at about the same time: No. 1018 (DEMONTS), No. 1041 (MEMBERTOU), and No. 1090 (DERAZILLY).

No. 999 was reassigned to Toronto in 1953. It is the only DAR steam locomotive to be preserved and now is on static display at the Canadian Railway Museum at Delson, Quebec.

The actual roster of D10s that were sold to the DAR was recorded in CPR files, and that list includes D10g No. 903, D10h Nos. 999, 1018, 1020, 1027, 1040, 1041, 1046, 1089, 1090, 1092, and 1111, and D10k Nos. 1067, 1077, and 1079.

CPR D10s loaned to the DAR; No. 1101 at Truro, 1950.

The roster of D10s that were loaned or leased to deal with short-term DAR traffic demands is clearer than that of the CP 500 class Ten-wheelers. Unlike the earlier temporary assignments of smaller CPR steam locomotives, the loans and leases of the D10s were much less frequent. Based on photographic evidence, statements in newspapers and other media, employee paper collections, and rail fan memorabilia and observations, the list includes D10b No. 929 and D10h Nos. 1015, 1038, 1050, and 1101.

The image of No. 1101, above, was taken at Truro in May 1950. Other photos of loaned/leased D10s can be seen as follows: No 1038 (pages 82 and 111) and No 1050 (page 91).

This right-side view of No. 1101 shows a variation of the reversing mechanisms used on steam locomotives. Beneath the raised section of the walkway on the side of No. 1101's boiler in front of the cab is the power reversing mechanism, which was a very different system compared to the reversing lever (Johnson bar) type. On page 58 the long rod is visible that emerges from the front of the engineer's side of the cab and angles downward along the boiler to connect to the reversing gear; this system was shown in the technical drawing (page x). A power reverse used compressed air to drive the mechanism while a Johnson bar relied on the engineer to move the linkage.

CPR G2 Pacifics, No. 2552, Truro, 1942.
GARY NESS COLLECTION

There were 166 CPR G2 Pacifics, Nos. 2500 to 2665. Only 7 of them were sold to the DAR, and these included G2p No. 2501; G2r Nos. 2511 (SUBERCASE), 2516, 2526; G2s Nos. 2551 and 2552 (HALIBURTON); and G2u No. 2629.

No. 2552, the first G2 sold to the DAR, still has its brass nameplate in this 1942 photograph at Truro. Two shops labourers appear to be cleaning the ashpan beneath the firebox. From the low angle of the sun it appears it could be late afternoon or evening, an indication that the locomotive may have arrived on Train 1 from Windsor, the daily-except-Sunday mixed train at 7:15 PM. The unlikely alternative is that it is being readied for Train 4, but that was the mixed Saturday-only train departing Truro at 5:25 PM; the corresponding opposite trains were morning operations at Truro. Also No. 2552 is facing east, which offers more evidence of an arrival in that direction. The confusing detail is the use of the white flags to either side of the stack, which suggest an extra train or perhaps a second section of the usual trains—a very likely occurrence during the busy World War Two years.

At this time the locomotive would have been resplendent with its maroon and black paint job, highlighted with gold pin striping, lettering, and numbering that was applied shortly after it arrived on the DAR in 1937.

Pacific No. 2551, Truro, 1958.
PATERSON-GEORGE COLLECTION

The first three CPR Pacifics, sold to the DAR in the late 1930s, were Nos. 2511, 2551, and 2552. They never received the enclosed vestibule or all-weather cabs that most of the G2 class received. On the DAR these three initially had their smoke boxes painted off-white, sported a number board with the Tuscan red paint, had gold pin stripes on the cylinders and domes, and had pin striping around logos and numbers on the tenders and cabs, respectively.

No.2551, above, was painted black with gold pinstripes in this September 10, 1958, scene in Truro. Interestingly, this photograph confirms this locomotive still had its open cab near the end of its career.

A winterization flap, which could be used to block drafts in the cab, is visible in this shot. The vestibule or all-weather cab was very popular with engine crews because it was warm in winter. (An example of a G2 with an all-weather cab is found on page 90.) The open cab visible here was exposed across the back, allowing swirling winds to whip around in the cab. The tent-like material is hanging in the retracted position just at the rear edge of the cab. This solution was only somewhat successful, and the open cabs were not well liked in winter.

IMAGES ON PAGES 60 AND 61 ▶

A fortunate phone call ended with an agreement to purchase these two exceptionally detailed 8x10 negatives. Both are rare, well exposed, highly detailed images inside the Kentville Machine Shop and reveal details few would ever see. There was no date or other data about the images.

The photograph on page 60 shows some of the huge machines, mostly lathes in this case, used for turning various locomotive components. The lathe to the rear appears to be designed for truing drive wheels.

The other photograph, on page 61, shows a common process in the shop during the steam era. There was always one steam locomotive receiving attention, usually involving complete disassembly to its component parts then rebuilding with new or refurbished parts.

There are various pieces of a locomotive visible here. Drive wheels are chained to the building support, preventing them from rolling away. The thin metal outer band or tire was removed from them using heat to expand the metal ring for removal. A new tire with a proper flange was heat-expanded, fitted, and then cooled to shrink it tightly onto the wheel. It is difficult to see if there are new tires on the two visible drive wheels since the flanges are shadowed. Other locomotive parts at the lower left include drive rods, a cowcatcher, truck wheels and axles on the floor in front of and behind the cowcatcher. The front bumper or pilot beam of the frame, on which the cowcatcher is mounted, is partially visible at centre left, above the cowcatcher and wheels. The rest of the locomotive's stripped frame likely was attached to it but it's out of the photograph's frame.

*Kentville
Machine Shop,
c. 1940.*

Kentville Machine Shop, c. 1940.
GARY NESS COLLECTION

*Train 11,
No. 470,
early 1940s,
Kingsport.*

HAROLD A.
JENKINS /
DOROTHY AND
JOE TAYLOR
COLLECTION

Train 11 had arrived from Kentville and was sitting, simmering quietly in the midday sun, at Kingsport, the northern terminus of the DAR's Kingsport Subdivision. The lull in activity was due to the crew's lunch break prior to turning the train. The date was shortly after No. 470's arrival in the early 1940s, given that the car in the picture is thought to be a 1937 or 1938 Chevrolet.

The CVR (the popular name for this line) had light rail, with a major load restriction on the bridge just north of Kentville at Mile 0.2 over the Cornwallis River (page 43). Light locomotives were needed to operate on the line. No. 470 had been sold to the DAR to replace small, aging DAR locomotives, such as Nos. 32 BLOMIDON and 33 GLOOSCAP and the CPR 500 series of 4-6-0 engines, which

also had been used on the CVR.

Engine crews recalled a particularly undesirable riding characteristic of No. 470. Its frame was narrow and the cab was high, creating the feeling that the locomotive swayed from side to side as it ambled along.

Near the end of the steam era, after No. 470 was scrapped, it was not uncommon to assign heavier locomotives to Train 13; although, any large engine was required to observe permanent slow orders of six miles per hour over the Cornwallis River bridge. Road switcher diesels travelled the Windsor Branch regularly without problems. Shortly after their arrival, however, business on the Branch diminished and much of it was abandoned.

Flanger No. 905.

DAR No. 5 VIOLA was a first-class coach that once belonged to the W&AR. The name VIOLA was dropped in 1911. The coach was built in 1890 and became DAR flanger 905 in 1938. It was renumbered No. 400400 as part of the CPR numbering system in 1958.

The device for which this flanger car is named was mounted on the body and frame at the right end on the car; there was a second blade at the other end. The old boarding platforms had been removed to accommodate the heavy support beams to which the plow blades are attached. The blades had to be raised and lowered to avoid snagging at level crossings. Each blade was notched to fit down over the rails to ensure that the top and sides of the rails were kept clear of ice. Careful study of the blade at right will reveal the notches.

A flanger was pushed ahead of a locomotive with the working blade shoving snow and ice to the sides. However, pushing a flanger, which had a lightweight car body, meant the snowfall had to be minimal. The flangers were ideal for their task; the interior of the old coaches could be kept warm for the operators who raised and lowered the blades based on trackside signs or whistle signals from the engineer. Also the passenger trucks ensured a smooth ride for the crew.

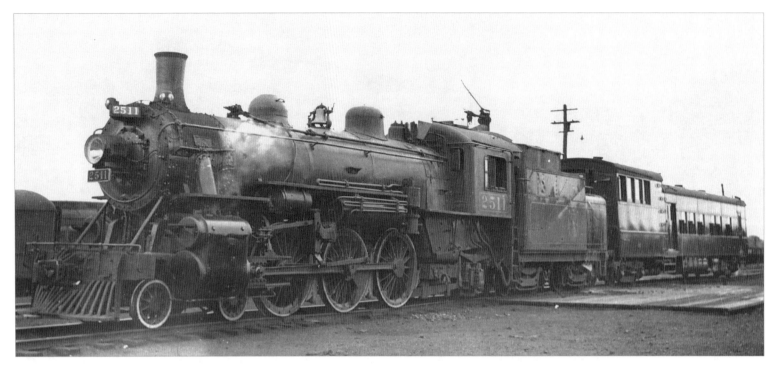

In July 1940 the CPR sent dynamometer car No. 62 to the DAR to conduct tests. Dynamometer cars, as the name implies, were equipped to test locomotive pulling power over a range of speeds. This testing then allowed the railway to determine a number of key factors, such as tonnage ratings and the loads a locomotive could pull at different speeds. A number of other factors, such as fuel efficiency, could also be determined.

The car's function relied on a piston connected to the coupler of the locomotive tender. This piston had a leather diaphragm and an enclosed glycerin-alcohol solution. This sophisticated apparatus was capable of dealing with drawbar pull up to 250 tons (steady pull) and buffer shock of 625 tons (sudden pull). The fluids in the piston transmitted pressures to pipes for measurement and recording on

devices in the forward compartment of the car. These recordings were then used to calculate locomotive performance.

A specially trained four-person crew accompanied the car: an equipment operator to monitor the readings, someone in the locomotive cab to communicate with the crew, and a cook.

On the occasion of this DAR visit, it was suggested the issue was about coal usage. Coal for steam locomotives required sieving for egg-size chunks. However, engine crews had noticed a lot of dust in their coal. This led to smaller bits of coal being pulled through the firebox and straight up the stack without burning, which was consistent with a higher coal usage. The dynamometer car data corroborated this observation, and the DAR initiated action to ensure that coal deliveries met standards precisely.

Morning school train approaching Kentville, 1942.

Ten-wheeler No. 44 was recorded on June 9, 1942, bringing a Kingsport–Kentville train into Kentville. From the sun's position in the photograph, this must be the morning Mixed Train 12, which brought schoolchildren to Kentville from various stops along the Kingsport Subdivision. The train left Kingsport at 7:20 AM, arriving at Kentville by 8:20 AM. The students were returned to their homes by a similar Mixed Train 13, which departed Kentville at 4:00 PM and arrived in Kingsport at 4:45 PM.

During the DAR's peak years in the mid-1930s, as many as twenty-two high school students regularly took the train to school. Tickets were specially priced for these passengers; books of tickets good for three months were available for $3.30.

The Kingsport Subdivision, although relatively short at 13.6 miles, was busy for many years. Even in the mid-1950s there were four scheduled mixed trains running daily, except on Sunday. In 1956 Train 11 left Kentville at 5:40 AM, and returned as Train 12 leaving Kingsport at 7:20 AM. The afternoon Trains, 13 and 14, followed a similar pattern, with Train 13 out of Kentville at 3:15 PM and Train 14 departing Kingsport at 4:05 PM.

The Weston Subdivision was built primarily for the shipment of apples. In the 1920s, it ran 14.5 miles from Centreville to Weston, had 5 stations and 12 warehouses for apples. The portion of the Kingsport Branch between Centreville and Kentville had 17 warehouses along that 4.8-mile length of track while the entire DAR had 121 such warehouses.

Business car NOVA SCOTIA, Kentville, June 1942.
HAROLD A. JENKINS

Today, the construction of new passenger train equipment would go unnoticed by newspapers, but in the early days of railways, everything that happened on the fledgling lines was reported. When the W&AR completed this wooden parlour car SANSPAREIL in 1896, an article described it as being outshopped in the well-known magenta colour of its first owner. In 1912 it was converted to a DAR business car for use by General Manager George Graham, and it was renamed NOVA SCOTIA. The car remained magenta until it was repainted in the CPR maroon sometime after 1918.

The car had a long and interesting career. It was parked at the North Street station during the Halifax explosion and luckily protected its occupants, the DAR general manager and his family. Graham contacted the DAR immediately and ordered a relief train, which brought medical and rescue personnel and equipment.

After the DAR Pontiac hi-railer arrived in 1957 (page 108), the CPR refitted the NOVA SCOTIA as business car No. 7 and assigned it to the superintendent of the Farnham Division, part of the Quebec District of the CPR. The declining use of business cars in the 1960s resulted in the sale of the No. 7 to the Upper Canada Railway Society and a return to the name, NOVA SCOTIA. It was sold to the London Ontario Historical Board c. 1969.

DAR cabooses No. 97 and No. 99 looked like typical cabooses, but the other cabooses rebuilt from DAR passenger cars, such as No. 91 above, looked like a cross between a caboose and the baggage car or the combine car that they originally were. For that reason, they were sometimes referred to as "combooses" by rail fans. The origin of the term is unknown, but it is quite descriptive and refers to the unusual half caboose half combine or baggage car appearance. DAR people never used the term; they knew them only as "vans," but they liked them.

No. 91 above was at Yarmouth on May 20, 1942, and was a good example of a comboose. It was based on an old DAR baggage-smoking combine coach No. 32 that was built in 1887. The cupola on top was added in 1923. After that, various histories for the car have been recorded. It has been suggested that No. 91 was rebuilt in 1941, but this photograph in 1942 appears to conflict with that assertion. An alternative version is that it remained much as it is here and was scrapped in 1955; although, it has also been suggested that it was sold and used as storage shed.

The other combooses were rebuilt from old coaches (No. 92), baggage cars (Nos. 97 and 99), and a combine car (No. 95). No. 98's origin is contentious and unclear; it has been suggested that it was converted from an old coach and in another case that an old baggage car was converted to a coach then to No 98.

When Dick George sent this photograph, he wrote a short caption on the back of it: "504 on the head-end. Riding in style! What would you pay for a ticket on this?" The date was June 8, 1942, and No. 504 had the daily, except Sunday, fast passenger Train 95 under way westbound out of Kentville in this wonderful recollection of DAR passenger service at its zenith.

The "Land of Evangeline" drumhead in the inset was proudly displayed on the rear of the awning-draped, open platform of the parlour-observation car GRAND PRE, and the passengers would have enjoyed the beauty of the Annapolis Valley, the Annapolis Basin, and the shores of the Bay of Fundy as the train made its way in a rather leisurely fashion to Digby and Yarmouth. Running time for the 145 miles from Kentville to Yarmouth was almost six hours; departure from Kentville was scheduled for 11:03 AM and arrival in Yarmouth at 4:50 PM. Regardless of the ride's duration, patrons loved this style of travel and spoke glowingly of the ambience of elegant rail travel through beautiful surroundings.

Ferry meet, Digby, 1942.
PATERSON-GEORGE COLLECTION

The importance of the Digby–Saint John ferry service to the CPR cannot be underestimated. As early as 1889 there was local contemplation that the CPR would be granted running rights to Halifax over the ICR main line. It was suggested that competition between the two major railways would ensure better quality service for freight and passengers. While Halifax and Dartmouth citizens and the CPR favoured such a permanent direct overland link, it was not to be. In 1910 the CPR made a final attempt to obtain running rights over the ICR into Halifax but Ottawa refused to co-operate; soon afterward the DAR was taken over by CPR.

CPR's purchase of the DAR included the important Digby–Saint John steamer service, which linked the DAR with CPR's trans-Canada main line, the Short Line from Montreal across Maine to Saint John. When CPR formally took over the Digby–Saint John ferry service on September 1, 1913, the CPR had at long last established its own, though indirect, through service from Montreal to Halifax.

In this photograph, taken at Digby on June 8, 1942, Train 98 has just arrived from Yarmouth and is in front of the station. Shortly it would be split and backed down onto the wharf in two sections for the scheduled meet with the DAR Digby–Saint John ferry, the *Princess Helene*. The ferry generally arrived at Digby at 11:00 AM, although the train was scheduled for 11:20 AM. The train would wait if the ferry was late.

*Digby wharf,
c. 1940.*
NOVA SCOTIA
DEPARTMENT OF
GOVERNMENT
SERVICES

Stories about old photographs sometimes surface by chance. When Doug Shaffner saw this undated photograph of the *Princess Helene* alongside the Digby wharf, he wrote to explain that he and other family members were convinced he was the little boy in the centre of the picture and the picture was taken in 1939 or 1940. Apparently, he and his mother, Mrs. Margaret Shaffner, were talking to the unidentified man while Doug's father was delivering business receipts and cash for the past three days to the purser of the *Princess Helene*. Doug's father was the McColl-Frontenac Oil Company (later Texaco) agent in Annapolis Royal. Normally he would deliver the money packet to Train 95 at Annapolis Royal for

transfer to the ferry and delivery by the CPR to the oil company's head office in Montreal. However, when the packet was not ready at train time, Mr. Shaffner drove to Digby to hand deliver it before the mid-afternoon departure.

The picture also shows the Digby switcher, D6a No. 519, working on the two tracks situated to the north side of the freight shed. The freight shed to the right of the train contained elevators for transferring materials between the ship and train. The elevator motor housings are visible projecting upward from the main roof of the freight shed. The track swinging across the wharf to the right was called the "T" track. Freight cars were loaded and unloaded on it.

CPR 0-6-0 Switcher No. 6227, Kentville, 1946. JAMES WALDER COLLECTION

On March 30, 1946, DAR No. 6227, a CPR class U3d 0-6-0 switcher was sitting quietly hissing steam at the water stand-pipe in Kentville yard. It was sold to the DAR in 1939 and served there until it was scrapped in 1957. Only one other CPR 0-6-0 was sold to the DAR, U3c No. 6189, which served from May 1937 to May 1939. Three other CPR 0-6-0s were loaned or leased briefly to the DAR prior to 1934: U2f No. 6058, U3a No. 6109 (page 35), and U3c No. 6161. These 0-6-0 switchers served primarily in Kentville and Yarmouth yard service.

Engine crews recall some interesting tales about these small lo-comotives. One night, No. 6227's crew—engineer Ralph Harvey and fireman Harley Cochrane—were ordered to push out of Kentville a heavy westbound train which was over-tonnage; they were surprised to discover that the train was already moving. They gave chase, but could not catch it. Equipped with small fifty-two-inch drivers, these 0-6-0s were designed for traction, not speed. Crews recall that the top recommended speed was only twenty miles per hour. No. 6227 returned to the station, and the westbound train and crew went obliviously on their way.

Referred to as the "Old Goat" by Kentville trainmen, No. 6227 was considered a good yard engine. On the flat, it could move heavy cuts of cars, such as the coal hoppers that frequently passed through Kentville off the Truro way freight. Coal shipped to Truro on the CNR from Sydney, Stellarton, and Springhill was distributed along much of the DAR line. Crewmen recall on one occasion the relative ease with which No. 6227 moved fourteen carloads of coal.

No. 470, one of a kind, Kentville. GEORGE PARKS

Over the years, the CPR sent a number of oddball or unusual steam locomotives to the DAR. These were very few in number and often were single representatives of their type in the roster. CPR D4 4-6-0 No. 470, former Quebec Central 4-6-0 No. 44 (page 54) and former G1 Pacific 4-6-2 No. 2209 (page 112) all fit that definition. Each of them was suited to a niche role within the railway. The two small 4-6-0 types were suited to runs on the CVR while the larger Pacific worked as a backup to the new diesels when a steam-drawn train was required in the last years of the steam to diesel transition. In this scene, No. 470 had assembled Train 11 in front of the Kentville station and was prepared to depart for its midday run to Kingsport.

No. 44 working as the Kentville switcher, late 1940s. GARY NESS COLLECTION

As mentioned earlier, the CPR sent a small number of 0-6-0 switchers to work at various sites, including Yarmouth, Digby, and Kentville. However, much more frequently, any available 4-6-0 was used as a switcher. Photographic evidence documented D6s and D10s in this role at various places. The image above shows the one-of-a-kind 4-6-0 ex-Quebec Central No. 44 in switching duties at Kentville. Note that the normal cowcatcher has been replaced with footboards for trainmen to stand on as they rode the front of the switcher while assembling trains in the yard. The locomotive was on the DAR from 1943 to 1954.

DAR caboose No. 97 was another version of the locally made cabooses that served on the DAR (page 67). In this 1946 photo, the
caboose was nearing the end of its days. It was scrapped in that
same year, and CPR standard cabooses would begin to arrive to
replace the DAR's aging homemade fleet.

Cabooses were in use on the ends of trains in Canada for a
very long time. The classic CPR offset cupola wood caboose could
be dated to 1905; however, cabooses existed long before that and
became common around 1880, when trainmen began to lobby collectively for improved working conditions. Air brakes did not yet
exist and conductors and trainmen were posted at stem-winder
brake-wheels, usually on the top of every fourth or fifth boxcar or
flatcar along a train. These men applied and released the brakes
at whistle signals from the locomotive. They were exposed to the
elements, and in cold weather their only respite was at stops when
they could gather in the locomotive cab or in a boxcar. Working
from the roof was also highly dangerous, so the first Canadian brake
vans were most welcome. These modified boxcars featured a brake-
wheel projecting up from the floor inside the car. From this simple
beginning the ubiquitous end-of-train van developed.

*Van 92,
Buy Victory
Bonds,
Kingston,
1945.*
R. ROBINSON

DAR van No. 92 was in Kingston, Nova Scotia, on May 9, 1945. The reason for its presence is unknown. The juxtaposition of the town adjacent to RCAF Station Greenwood and the advertisement of Victory Bonds is interesting.

Half of Canada's World War Two costs were covered by selling War Savings Certificates and Victory Bonds. Of the two, Victory Bonds were far more successful in raising money for the war effort. Drives took place every six months throughout the war. These were widely advertised on the radio and in the mail and newspapers. Posters also played a prominent role as is evident here. The ten wartime drives raised $12.5 billion.

In addition to serving RCAF Station Greenwood near Kingston, the DAR also served RCAF Station Stanley, at Stanley; HMCS Cornwallis, a Royal Canadian Navy Operations/Training base on the shore of the Annapolis Basin; and Aldershot Military Camp, just to the north of Kentville. In addition to serving the naval port at Cornwallis, the DAR served two other naval operations ports: Digby and Yarmouth. The DAR also served the World War Two troop marshalling camp at Windsor.

Train 97 with No. 999 in the Halifax Cut.

This image is without data but must have been taken prior to July 1953, when D10 No. 999 left the DAR. Since it arrived in 1937, the dates do not offer much evidence about this photo.

The train is the scheduled Mixed Train 97 under way westbound in the Halifax Cut away from the CN Halifax station. The train does not have any freight cars yet; they will be added behind the locomotive at the CNR Rockingham yard.

It was very unusual for a D10 to lead this train. Normally a G2 Pacific would be assigned. The latter were faster, rode more smoothly, and had more power. Nonetheless engineers considered the DAR D10s to be good locomotives—except for two of them, D10s Nos. 999 and 1090, which were hated. They had a Johnson bar reverse lever mechanism, which was very unpopular in any comparison to the more common and easy-to-use screw reverse and air reverse mechanisms. Each of these three types of devices controlled steam input into the upper piston valve, which in turn determined direction of travel by injecting steam into the lower drive piston (page x). The screw reverse mechanism looked like a metal steering wheel in front of the engineer; it was spun easily by one hand. An air reverse mechanism used air pressure and was easiest of all to operate, although the screw reverse was considered more precise. The Johnson bar was a large vertical lever in front of the engineer. It took some effort to pull or push and it was not precise.

Caboose No. 99 on a work train, Canning, 1945.

This scene occurred near Canning on the Cornwallis Subdivision in March 1945. Work Extra 555 had No. 555 on the head end, a ballast car in tow, and DAR caboose No. 99 at the rear.

There is little about this caboose to indicate its origin, except for the passenger trucks. The caboose was built by the DAR using an old DAR baggage car, No. 56, which had been built in 1897 by Rhodes Curry in Amherst, Nova Scotia. The repurposing of the old car made good sense because the passenger trucks ensured a smooth ride. The rebuilding as a van occurred in Kentville in 1921. It was scrapped in 1946, after serving as an integral part of the DAR caboose fleet in the 1920–1940 era.

A newspaper article dated April 13, 1923, offered some insight about what the new No. 99 might have looked like. The article is about caboose No. 96 but states that this series of rebuilds was "uniformly fitted and comfortable." The author asserts, "Manager Graham certainly sees to it that the freight crews, when out on the road are comfortable." The car is described as "a palace on wheels." The "hurricane deck" (cupola) was fitted with "plush upholstered tip-seats with iron frames." The interior included a heater, cookstove, iron couch frames, mattresses and bedding in a bedding locker, a table on hinges on the wall, a desk, pantry, and clothes locker. The exterior of the car was painted "light red" and the interior was a "darker colour."

This February 1945 snowplow extra train has just arrived in Truro after an uneventful run from Windsor. Given what could happen on eventful runs, this was a blessing.

One of the more action-packed stories about the DAR snow-plow trains featured a runaway locomotive in early February 1905. A heavy snowfall was threatening to close the western sections of the DAR. No 19 OBERON, a small 4-4-0, and a snowplow left Annapolis around 5:00 PM bound for Yarmouth. About 6:10 PM the locomotive ran through Digby at full speed, losing parts of its cab on a street. A while later the engineer limped into the station to inquire if anyone had seen his locomotive. The snowplow had derailed at Gilpin Crossing and turned on its side, allowing the locomotive to continue but with a very damaged cab. Unfortunately, the engineer had been thrown from his window; he was holding the throttle at the time and his clothing must have pulled it wide open as he exited the cab. He was dragged a short distance in the debris and then thrown free. Concerned about others, he walked on an injured foot about a half mile to the station. Meanwhile, the fireman managed to crawl forward from the tender and bring the locomotive to a stop about a quarter mile west of Digby. How the fireman got on the tender is unclear, but his side of the cab was destroyed. He walked back to the station, and another locomotive was sent to tow No. 19 back to Digby.

Snowplow operation, 1947.
GARY NESS COLLECTION

DAR plow No. 909, an early wood plow, was awaiting its next call while parked on a siding at Kentville in 1947. Many details—often hidden under snow—are revealed in this photograph. The large plowing surface was sculpted to lift the snow and throw it up and off to the sides when operating at sufficient speed.

Careful inspection shows that the lower leading edge of the plow had two parts: the heavy steel edges fixed to both sides and a movable heavy steel centre section. The movable part was for flanging, the removal of snow between the rails. The flanging surface was controlled by one of the two-man plow crew; the second man was a spotter whose job was to spot trackside signs indicating an approaching level crossing or switch, in which case he ordered the flanger blade raised. Failure to do so resulted in heavy damage to the planking and roadway between the rails at level crossings and some risk to the plow crew, who were seated in the cupola atop the plow. The two heavy metal rods attached to the top on the flanger were clearly visible below and to either side of the coupler. The plow crew also had to communicate with the locomotive crew whose members were literally running blind when the plow was throwing snow. This was done with whistle signals prior to the advent of radios.

The wings with Service 909 lettering also moved; here they are retracted. The plow operated with the wings retracted until deep drifts were cleared; afterwards the wings were spread in stages to widen the cut.

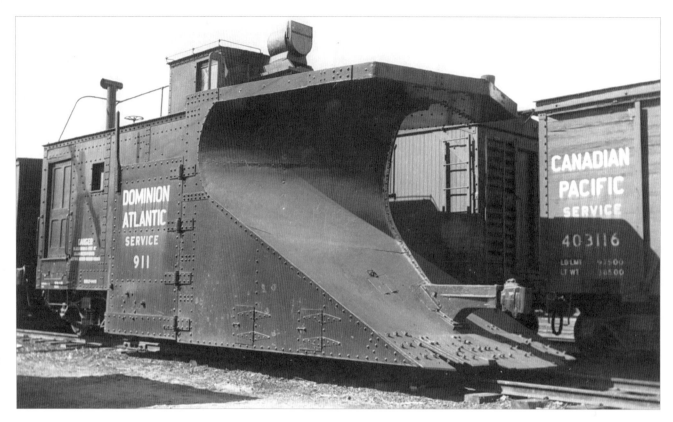

Modern snowplow details, No. 911.

This more modern steel plow had much the same features visible on page 79, except it was a much heavier and more durable plow, hence less prone to damage and derailment.

The Kingsport line was known for really long snowdrifts between Centreville and Weston. Since it was not the main line, snow trains were sent with two locomotives, freight cars, and a caboose behind the plow. The train would work to Weston, picking up and delivering freight cars to sidings and clearing snow as needed. The front locomotive would cut off from the second locomotive as needed and plow drifts. If it made it through a drift, the second locomotive would bring the train up to the first locomotive and the train would proceed. If the plow was stopped, the second locomotive cut off, and pulled the first locomotive and plow back for another pass at the drift.

Gerry Parks recalled a Sunday afternoon run, which left Kentville bound for Kingsport. There was a little snow in Kentville, but only one locomotive was pushing the plow, which had Gerald Comeau in control. At the Kingsman Cut near Pereau, the steam locomotive and plow bogged down in drift that was up to the fireman's window; they were stuck for eight hours before a light locomotive (running without cars) could be sent. The two locomotives then combined to punch through the drift.

Snowplow train, late 1950s.
P. BISHOP / GARY NESS COLLECTION

Older newspaper stories about the DAR snow closures abound. For example, in 1923 a series of severe February snowstorms followed by a thaw and then a freeze shut down the Midland for two full days. Ice on the rails could not be removed, and a plow and large crew of men that departed Kentville did not arrive in Truro by the next day. The telegraph wires were down and the men were not heard from for over twenty-four hours. This closure led to a coal shortage for locomotives in the Valley and a special DAR coal train was marshalled in Truro and sent over CNR tracks to Windsor Junction to access the DAR line.

The snow blockade that began February 20, 1905, was arguably the worst of many challenging situations. It started with telegraph wires down and the entire line blocked with snow; soon entire towns were shut down. There was no coal for trains or homes; neighbours shared food and buckets of coal with those in need. Farmers lacked water for their livestock and wood for heat. The DAR enlisted the help of citizens, including students, to clear the lines, much of which required lots of manpower and machines to chip away the ice; progress was slow. It was March 3 when the eastern part of the line reopened. The western end's troubles continued with daytime thaws followed by nightly freezing. It was March 10—eighteen days from the start of the blockade—when the papers declared the line open again.

D10
No. 1038
switching,
Brooklyn.
ROBERT
TAYLOR

During the 1950s, Friday was called "pig day" because the Kentville–Windsor–Truro freight trains picked up a number of stock cars loaded with hogs destined for Truro. Port Williams, Windsor, Brooklyn, and Kennetcook were involved. Sometimes Train 100 would pick up loads at Middleton; these would be added to the run to Windsor before departing Kentville.

This photograph of D10h Ten-wheeler No. 1038 switching at Brooklyn shows a typical hog train. The locomotive was not displaying white flags alongside the stack, thus it was not an extra train. Likely it was Train 5 northbound from Windsor to Truro. In front of No. 1038 and the CNR boxcar, there is at least one stock car

(just out of the picture at the right). A large hog pen was located beside the spur at that point. The CNR boxcar was probably being unloaded at the tall Co-op mill behind No. 1038. At that time, it was common to deliver bulk grain shipments to the mill in boxcars. The mill used the grains to manufacture various feeds for local farmers.

Brooklyn did not have a passing track, and crews confronted a facing-point spur, requiring jigging or on the fly switch movements, described on page 41, to remove the hog cars from the spur and insert them behind the locomotive. Then the CNR boxcar had to be repositioned in front of the locomotive and moved back at the mill to finish unloading.

No. 2528 approaching Bear River bridge.

Taken from the elevated embankment of old Highway No. 1, which paralleled the tracks and could be seen at the upper left, this photograph captures the scenic beauty of the Annapolis Basin. The site has been described in DAR literature as "one of the most photogenic in the East," and numerous photographs were taken here in the 1940s, 1950s, and 1960s. Unfortunately, by the 1970s a copse of fast-growing poplar trees had grown on the slope above the railway, mostly obscuring the view.

The site was just to the west of the Bear River bridge, approximately seven miles east of Digby. The Digby Gap, through which the Saint John ferry sails, was visible in the distance.

The absence of exhaust from the stack indicates that the engineer was making the required stop before crossing the bridge. Bear River bridge was one of four drawbridges on the DAR; the others were at Weymouth, Clementsport, and the Shubenacadie River. All four bridges had central swing sections with special rules governing crossings. On the signal of the bridge tender, the train was required to cross at fifteen miles per hour.

This picture had been arranged. The photographer signalled the engineer to whistle and he did; the whistle was releasing steam on the right side of the top of the boiler. The scene is more dramatic by the fact that the pops, the pressure safety valve, also released excess steam pressure on the left side of the locomotive's boiler.

Preparing a steam engine for the road. JAMES WALDER COLLECTION

This photo of No. 2551 at Kentville shows the locomotive being prepared for its next run. In addition to filling the tender with coal and water, there were a number of other routine chores to complete before the engine was again ready for the road. Here we see a round-house worker, Carl Smith, cleaning out the ashpan beneath the firebox. Ash and cinders (clinker) from the burning of coal would drop down through a grate (page xi), which formed the bottom of the firebox. In addition to allowing ashes and cinders to drop into the ashpan, the grate also allowed air to reach the fire from below.

Obviously red-hot cinders could not be allowed to drop onto the railbed, which when it did occur, started fires in the ties. This was a particular concern on the railway's many wood trestles and bridges. Accidental fires from this source were frequent enough that all the big bridges were protected by a bridge tender who walked the bridge after every steam locomotive had crossed.

The workman in this case had coupled an air hose to a ground pipe and was using air pressure to blow out the ashpan. The tap for the line can be seen near the man's right lower leg.

Large piles of cinders would accumulate in the area, but the railways had the perfect solution (page 117): a crane would load the cinders into gondola cars, which would be distributed in work trains so the cinders could be dumped as ballast on the railbed.

Gypsum train crossing the Avon River, Windsor, mid-1950s.

A double-headed gypsum train, drawn by D10h Ten-wheelers Nos. 1092 and 999, was westbound onto the bridge across the Avon River at Windsor, Nova Scotia, when this photo was captured sometime in the mid-1950s. This image, and the one following, shows a major feature of the DAR: large bridges. The railway ran parallel to the Bay of Fundy coastline for much of its length; therefore, numerous river estuaries were crossed. This would not be remarkable but for the twice daily tides of the Bay of Fundy, which average thirty-five feet in the Minas Basin. For miles inland from the coast, rivers rose and fell with the tides, creating wide flood plains on either side of even the smallest rivers. The tide in this picture is on its way out.

Before low tide is reached, the river will have dropped much further, leaving a stream approximately one hundred feet across! The high-tide marks were visible on the wooden planking of the bridge piers.

Besides the corrosive effects of saltwater spray on metal bridges, the tidal movements shifted enormous volumes of water that was reddish and turbid, laden with silt picked up by the strong currents in the shifting waters. This bridge's piers or foundations were sunk deep into the sandy river bottom and had to endure large forces as the enormous amounts of water shifted in and out of the rivers with the tides. Shifting ice floes in the winter months compounded the problem, hence the metal sheathing on all edges of the piers of this bridge.

D10 derailed,
Windsor,
c. 1950.

An interested crowd had gathered to see derailed D10 No. 1092, and the big hook with its work train. The locomotive was on the main line to Halifax, and it appears that its wheels split the switch to the siding in the foreground. It served the Windsor Plaster Company; Lawtons Drugs occupies that site now. The distant workmen on the tracks in front of the heavy crane appear to be examining that piece of track and the switch point before rolling the crane forward to begin lifting.

The waterfront area along the St. Croix River in the background was quite busy in the steam era. At the left, above the line of railway telegraph poles, is the flat-roofed textile plant. In the background at the right are a group of buildings that the DAR accessed on a long spur off the Truro Subdivison. The buildings included the Colonial Fertilizer plant (formerly the Pidgeon Fertilizer plant) and the Colonial Hide plant (for tanning hides and making soap), both owned by the Corenco Rendering Company of Boston. During the fertilizer season in the late 1930s, almost daily the DAR would dispatch a locomotive to the busy fertilizer plant to do switching and take loads to Kentville for distribution in regular trains.

A large military base once occupied the open space between the train and the industries. This was a troop marshalling area that could host ten thousand men awaiting convoys to take them to Europe. It was purpose-built in the early war years and was gone by the early 1950s.

Nose to nose.
GARY NESS COLLECTION

This undated photograph shows Pacific No. 2627 nose to nose with an unidentified D10 Ten-wheeler. This is another of those imaginative shots that is interesting because it is outside the box. The engines are standing on the track beside the coaling tower and the sanding tower. One can surmise from other photos showing the two towers and their relative positions (page 114) that the D10 was very likely in position to load coal. The upright posts to the left of No. 2627 are the legs of the sanding tower. The track in the left foreground was for hoppers to deliver coal to the coaling tower (page 115).

Study of other details in the background reveals an open door to a roundhouse stall and the turntable aligned to the track these two locomotives occupy. One can only conclude that No. 2627 had either just left the roundhouse, or more likely, was about to be put into the roundhouse. Normally coal would be loaded after a trip to ensure its availability while the locomotive simmered away until its next assignment.

G2 No. 2552 on Bear River bridge, early 1950s.
NOVA SCOTIA DEPARTMENT OF GOVERNMENT SERVICES

The employees' operating timetable specified a permanent slow order of fifteen miles per hour across the Bear River bridge. Pacific No. 2552 was almost across and would have been accelerating toward Digby with westbound Passenger Train 95 in this c. 1950 scene.

Many railway stories focus on the more glamorous railway jobs in the running trades. There were many other critical jobs that usually went unnoticed. One example is the job of bridge tenders. The scene in this photograph reveals the bridge tender's shed to the right and just ahead of the locomotive. Bridge tenders operated the swing section of the drawbridge, which was built to accommodate high-masted boat traffic. The lateral projections under the near end of the bridge are visible, and the round abutment in the centre of the swing section is also visible on close inspection.

Since hot cinders dropped by a steam locomotive could set fire to creosoted timbers, bridge tenders also made walking inspections of the entire length of the bridge after every train. If they found a hot spot, they scooped water from the barrels positioned at regular intervals across the top of the bridge.

It was also customary to walk the bridge before scheduled trains arrived. This part of the job required agility and no doubt created some anxious moments when a train appeared early. The bridge tender would have to run for it and if he was likely to be overtaken, his only recourse was to squeeze up against a convenient water barrel as the train passed. Ice on the ties also made life interesting.

Train and ferry meet on the dock at Yarmouth.
NOVA SCOTIA DEPARTMENT OF GOVERNMENT SERVICES

Yarmouth shipbuilders and owners were quick to discern that an Annapolis Valley rail system with associated steamship connections would provide freight for their ships, but they also had visions of future passenger traffic from New England to Nova Scotia.

In the early 1900s, tourism became an important business due to its promotion by the DAR and CPR in New England and Canada. In particular, the Annapolis Valley was considered a major tourist attraction as attested in the following excerpt from the *Halifax Herald*, dated October 31, 1923.

As a tourist Paradise, the Annapolis Valley, popularly known as "The Land of Evangeline" made famous by Longfellow's "Evangeline," is now visited yearly by many thousands of American and Canadian tourists. The Annapolis Valley contains within its bounds many points of more than passing interest. The Digby Basin, Fort Anne, Annapolis Royal with is treasure of antique relics gathered in the ancient officer's barracks, the Cornwallis Valley, Gaspereau, Minas Basin, the Look-off, the Avon, and last but (CONTINUED NEXT PAGE)

not least beautiful Grand Pre [sic] Park, form so many points of scenic beauty, historical lore, and particular interest to visitors, that the writer feels incapable of describing them adequately. One must see this alluring country to fully appreciate its un-surpassed scenery. The panorama from the Look-off is a scene never to be forgotten.

Such was the volume of tourist traffic that in the DAR's heyday, this small CPR subsidiary became nearly as multi-dimensional as its much larger parent. Besides operating is own rail and steamship services, the DAR also owned three luxury hotels. Designed to ac-commodate tourists to the Annapolis Valley, the Lakeside Inn at Lake Milo in Yarmouth and the Pines Hotel in Digby were open during the tourist season; the Cornwallis Inn in Kentville was open year-round.

Train 98, the daily-except-Sunday first-class day Express Passenger from Yarmouth to Halifax, was the premier DAR pas-senger train of its day and was advertised by the DAR as "air condi-tioned Buffet-Parlor and day coach service." This August 20, 1954, photograph captured some of the normal activities of the train prior to its scheduled 9:05 AM departure for Halifax. The entire train had been backed onto the Yarmouth wharf about a half mile west of the station to meet the Boston–Yarmouth ferry. The backing move was accomplished with the train's road engine, Pacific No. 2617, coupled to the first coach of the train. The baggage and express cars were temporarily at the rear of the consist for the train and ferry meet to allow efficient transfer of baggage. Before departure the baggage cars would be shunted to situate the baggage and express cars between the locomotive and the passenger cars.

This photograph, taken inside the Kentville round-house, shows D10 No. 1050 sitting in the fourth stall next to three other DAR locomotives. D10 No. 1111 sits next to No. 1050. No. 1111 was the last of the 502 D10s built by CPR; DAR employees popularly called it the "Four Aces." Sent to the DAR in January 1954, it was scrapped in March 1959 after a brief but colourful stay. While hauling the Annapolis Royal–Yarmouth way freight on July 19, 1956, it was in collision with the Digby yard engine, D10 No. 1015. Although the crews were uninjured, both locomotives were extensively damaged. They were repaired in the Kentville shops.

Kentville roundhouse was the major engine servicing and turning facility on the DAR. Locomotives could be turned on wyes at Annapolis Royal, Digby, Yarmouth, and Windsor, and they were given routine servicing, such as coaling, watering, and lubrication at numerous sites, but only in Kentville were major class 1, 2, or 3 repairs done. Kentville's roundhouse was equipped with a machine shop, and during the 1950s seven blacksmiths with seven helpers were employed full-time. Class 3 repairs involved a general inspection for wear; any leaks were corrected. Class 2 repairs involved such work as relining the boiler with new tubes, replacing the firebrick in the firebox, turning the tires on a lathe, overhauling the ashpans (making these tighter fitting to avoid dropping embers on wooden bridges), and replacing the "brasses," which refer to the crankpins extending out from locomotive's drive wheels and to which the side rods connect. Class 1 repairs were the most serious. Simply put, the locomotive was stripped to its frame and completely rebuilt.

Inspection car M-107, Kentville, mid-1950s.
BOB BROOKS

The caption on the reverse of this staged photograph reads, "Train orders being delivered to Extra M-107 East prior to departure Yarmouth." The gentleman reading the train orders is J. C. McCuaig, manager of the DAR. Others in the photo include driver Vince Young (secretary), passenger C. E. Haystead (roadmaster), at the far right Reg McGill (general agent, Yarmouth), and second from the right Jack McQuarrie (engineer). An examination of the recorded years of DAR service of these five individuals and the dates of their career advancements, reasonably suggests the date of this photograph was sometime in the mid-1950s.

M-107 was a CPR designation applied to a succession of official touring cars, which were used by the "brass," DAR management or CPR officials from Montreal, for inspections of the line. In this case, M-107 is a 1938 McLaughlin-Buick limousine with a wind-up glass privacy barrier behind the driver's seat It was restricted to the rails and was specially equipped for its duties: flanged wheels, a bell, air horns, footboards, a number-board, and pilot are all obvious additions. The small pipe aimed at the rail immediately ahead of the front wheel was for sand application to the rail in the event that the wheels lost traction during starts or on a hill. The cylinder visible beneath the driver is an air reservoir.

The removable white flags displayed on either side ahead of the front fenders signify that the car will run as an extra, an unscheduled operation.

CPR G2 Pacifics loaned to the DAR, No. 2528, Kentville, 1956.
ROBERT SANDUSKY

The loan or lease of the G2 class locomotives—like the D10 class—was infrequent. Knowledge of their presence on the DAR is based on some direct evidence, such as photographs, formal papers, and reports, and indirectly from rail fan memorabilia and observations. The list includes G2p Nos. 2500, 2505; G2r No. 2515; G2s Nos. 2526 and 2528 (above); and G2u Nos. 2617 (page 94), 2627 (known to have been given DAR markings), and 2665 (page 96).

Interestingly, Omer Lavallée's book did not include No. 2528 in the list of temporary visitors to the DAR. That's because the photo above at Kentville is one of only a very few. This one would not have been made public if Robert (Bob) did not know about that paucity of evidence; he decided to send it along with another image that I had requested. Bob related that on June 28, 1956, he and some companions took the mixed train to Kentville, en route to Digby. The mixed train to Kentville was pulled by No. 2551, which upon arrival at Kentville was uncoupled. No 2528 was taking on water prior to taking over Train 95 from Pacific No. 2627. One can see the line on No. 2528's tender, which shows wetness (condensation due to the cold water) on the lower part of the tender. The coal bunker is above and in front of the darker wet area. Bob and his friends took Train 95 behind No. 2528 to Digby, where Bob would photograph the Governor General's special train (page 106).

CHAPTER 5

THE DAR/CPR ERA: THE STEAM TO DIESEL TRANSITION 1956–1960

*Derailment
of Pacific
No. 2617,
Aldershot,
1956.*
HAROLD BAILEY

Cyril White Sr. was the engineer when No. 2617 left the rails and plowed its nose into the sand near Camp Aldershot, just north of Kentville. He jokingly admitted he thought it would never stop burrowing deeper, but when it finally did, he stepped out the cab window onto the ground. The reason for this 1956 derailment was likely a switch point being picked (split) by a drive wheel of the locomotive; although, other potential causes were present.

We know that the train was headed back to Kentville and would not have taken the spur at the left. The track on which it should have travelled is visible in the next photograph and shows the torn-up main line to the side of No. 2617. This indicated that the switch was aligned for the through track, not the siding. Another clue pointing to a picked switch is apparent beneath the locomotive number on the cab, where a piece of badly mangled rail from the siding is visible. Other evidence is beneath the tender where pieces of the switch frog were to be found. The frog is that specialized piece of track forming an "X" to allow wheels to cross another rail as they move through the switch. All the visible evidence seemed to suggest that the locomotive was misdirected to the right toward the siding and off the rails. Other factors were also at play.

(CONTINUED NEXT PAGE)

Derailment of Pacific No. 2617, Aldershot, 1956.

HAROLD BAILEY

A G2 Pacific was heavy for the Kingsport line. Its weight could have caused a rail to spread or roll over. This is why lighter locomotives were normally assigned to this run. Apparently, the usual smaller D10 Ten-wheeler was unavailable, and when No. 2617 arrived in Kentville it could be readied quickly, so it was dispatched north over the light rail of the Kingsport Subdivision. It would have crept along at the slow pace required of a large engine and was only a few miles from ending its return leg to Kentville when the derailment happened.

The final possibility is a sharpened flange on the locomotive's right-hand side. Excessive wear produced a sharp edge on the flange, which could slide between the switch points causing this kind of mishap. However, flange wear was normally monitored carefully. This was the end of the steam era, and steam engines may have gone longer between complete overhauls.

It would be difficult to ascertain whether either of the latter two possibilities applies since all the damage to the rail cannot be seen in these photographs. A turned-over rail would have to be out of view behind and under the tender and first car. Similarly, the presence of a sharp flange cannot be determined. Even though we have a clear view of the locomotive's underside, we cannot see the right-hand front drive wheel, which could be the culprit.

Roger Robinson was one of the photographers hired by the CPR to take publicity shots of new Dayliner No. 9058. He worked along the DAR during the week prior to the official commencement of Dayliner service, and luckily he did not confine his activities to the Dayliner. Realizing the significance of the last official days of steam-drawn passenger trains on the DAR, he recorded these excellent scenes of Train 98 at Digby and meeting Train 95, its westbound counterpart at Annapolis Royal. These particular photographs were taken on Friday August 19, 1956. The final day of scheduled operation of steam-hauled passenger service occurred eight days later on Saturday August 18, 1956.

The above image of Train 98, the first-class fast passenger train from Yarmouth to Halifax, had arrived at Digby at 12:30 PM and No. 2665 was backing the head end of the train (mail, baggage, and express cars) onto the wharf for the scheduled meet with the inbound ferry, the *Princess Helene*, from Saint John. The Digby yard engine, usually a D10 Ten-wheeler, would back the rear portion of the train, usually two passenger coaches and a parlour-observation car, onto a separate spur on the wharf for the exchange of passengers. The reassembled train would depart eastbound exactly thirty minutes later at 1:00 PM.

Trains 98 and 95 meet.
ROGER ROBINSON / CP PHOTOGRAPHIC SERVICES NEG. NO. 25351

The 1956 timetable called for a 2:02 PM meet between the two premier DAR Passenger Trains 98 and 95 at Round Hill, 26.1 miles east of Digby; however, it was common for Train 98 to be late. Trainmen of the day recall that the scheduled meet occurred only once or twice a week at the assigned point. More frequently, and shown in this photograph, the trains passed at Annapolis Royal, 5.9 miles west of Round Hill. This frequent ten- to twenty-minute tardiness of Train 98 was attributable to scheduling of 98's on-time performance based on connections with Train 40 eastbound out of Montreal. Thus, this meet at Round Hill was dependent upon on-time departure from Montreal and arrival in Saint John, New Brunswick—and integration with the ferry in both Saint John and Digby. Such close adherence to timetable was quite good, all considered.

Train 95, led by Pacific No. 2617, is in the hole (in the passing siding) for the meet. Train 98, pulled by Pacific No. 2665, is the superior train due to its eastbound direction, and based on its running rights in the rules it is continuing along the main line. Trains were assigned superiority by train order, superior class (conferred by the operating timetable), or by superior direction.

The three crew members seen leaning out of various parts of the head end of the stopped train were required, as part of the Canadian Uniform Code of Operating Rules, to perform a visual inspection of Train 98 as it passed. Undoubtedly another crew member was standing on the opposite side of Train 98's track to scan the right side of the train for any irregularities.

Last week of steam-drawn Train 98, Kentville, 1956.
HAROLD BAILEY

Train 98 from Yarmouth was waiting at Kentville station for its scheduled 4:05 PM departure to Halifax on Tuesday, August 14, 1956, during the last week of operation of steam-powered Trains 95, 96, 97, and 98. On Saturday, August 18, 1956, each of these trains made their final trip, and on Monday, August 20, two Dayliners running on faster schedules replaced them.

Prior to August 1956, the DAR's regular main line passenger service included six scheduled trains: two fast Passenger Trains 98 and 95 and four Mixed Trains 96, 97, 99, and 100. Mixed trains had both freight and passenger cars in their consist. By convention, eastbound trains were even-numbered and superior and westbound trains were odd-numbered and inferior. The terms *superior* and

inferior indicate that westbound trains, those moving in the Halifax to Yarmouth direction, must take the siding at meets with scheduled eastbound trains.

For many years, a typical consist for Train 98 included a mail car, two express cars that were picked up in Digby, a baggage car, two coaches, and a parlour car complete with chairs on the awning-covered, open observation platform at the rear. However, in the brief period just prior to the inauguration of Dayliner service, the express cars were taken off Trains 95 and 98 and were placed on the Mixed Trains 99 and 100. For that reason, there were no express cars in Train 98's consist. Instead there were two baggage cars flanking a mail car.

Last run of Train 97 Kentville, 1956.
HAROLD BAILEY

The DAR notified Kentville professional photographer Harold Bailey that the last official steam-hauled passenger run was on Saturday August 18, 1956. This particular run was historic for several reasons, not the least of which was that it had operated for almost fifty years, beginning c. 1907, when it was called the Express Daily from Halifax to Kentville. It was a mixed train: the combination passenger/baggage car is just visible at the rear of the train as the locomotive cleared Aberdeen Street prior to stopping, with the combination car spotted alongside the Kentville station platform for passengers to disembark.

Trains 95 and 98, the scheduled fast passenger runs, had completed their final trips between Yarmouth and Halifax earlier on this Saturday. Train 97, shown here, left Halifax on Saturday on time at 2:15 PM, arriving at Kentville at 5:45 PM. This protracted schedule (three and one half hours) for a mixed train allowed for setting out and picking up freight cars along the route.

On this day, there were more crew members than passengers when the train left Halifax with three people bound for Beaver Bank and Mount Uniacke. Conductor Waldo Crosby was in charge of the train and rode in the passenger compartment of the combination car, as did trainman M. W. Alexander. The baggage compartment crew included a baggage man, Alvin (Cy) Gates; engineer Arthur (Jigs) Ells, and fireman George Goucher were on the head end.

ALCO S3
diesel's arrival,
Kentville, 1956.
HAROLD BAILEY

Compared with the rest of the Canadian Pacific's system, the DAR was quite late in replacing steam with diesel locomotives. It was July 1, 1956, when diesels made their first appearance on the DAR. Montreal Locomotive Works (ALCO) S3 switchers Nos. 6560 and 6561 sat in front of the Kentville station while being inspected by George Bishop, Kentville office manager (third from right) and Ray Christie, DAR master mechanic (far right). The other two gentlemen are thought to be representatives from Montreal Locomotive Works who had accompanied the new units to Nova Scotia.

These locomotives were unique in at least two ways. They were the only CPR switchers that came from the manufacturer with multiple unit controls and an electrical system allowing the two locomotives to be controlled by one engineer. The diesels were also distinguished by their lettering—they were the only diesels ever to bear the Dominion Atlantic lettering. In fact, they are thought to be the only diesels ever lettered with the name of a Canadian Pacific subsidiary line.

These two diesels originally were intended to replace double- and even triple-headed steam motive power on the lucrative gypsum trains between Dimock's and Hantsport. However, the two S3 diesels proved to be too light for this service, even though they pulled only twenty-car trains. The S3s then appeared together or as separate units in a variety of other services over the entire DAR system until they were replaced by SW1200rs diesels in 1959.

S3s refuelling at Windsor.
GARY NESS COLLECTION

After their arrival at Kentville on July 1, 1956, the two S3 diesels were moved to Windsor and put to work on the gypsum runs. Initially, there were no refuelling tanks at any point on the line, and for a time Arthur Murdoch of Imperial Oil was called frequently to the Windsor yard to refill Nos. 6560 and 6561 from his truck. A tank was installed shortly afterwards at Windsor.

The ALCOs, as these diesels were often called, proved to be underpowered and too light for service on the heavy gypsum runs. Even the addition of plates of lead ballast on their running boards did not change their performance sufficiently, and in 1959 they were replaced by the more powerful SW1200rs diesels, the mainstay of the DAR fleet for the next three decades. In the early 1960s, Nos.

6560 and 6561 worked in Thunder Bay, where they continued to operate with multiple unit control ("MU'd" is the common railway jargon). Later these diesels were transferred further west to Moose Jaw, where both units served until they were involved in accidents that ended their careers. No. 6560 hit SD40-2 No. 5942 on September 23, 1981. Moved to Weston Shops, the unit was officially retired on May 18, 1982. No. 6561 was in a yard accident at Moose Jaw on January 21, 1983. It was officially retired from the company records on May 16, 1983, and moved on June 9, 1983, to Weston Shops to be stripped for parts. The unit entered the shops on October 20, 1983, and was scrapped.

The two ALCO S3 diesel-electrics arrived on the system and were displayed first, at Kentville, and then moved to Windsor, their permanent base. There was a lot of interest in this new type of locomotive. These photographs at Windsor show some of the people who inspected them. In both examples, there are men on the running boards and careful examination will reveal men in the cabs. One would hope that the young man clambering onto No. 6561 was being supervised by the adult peering around the front of the long hood of the diesel.

The S3's short-lived time on the DAR resulted in a limited number of photographs of these diesels, especially after they went into service. Luckily, an unknown photographer recorded these two scenes and they were saved.

I was given an envelope containing two negatives; they were obviously done one after the other by one person, but I have been unable to discover who that might be. The prints are from high-quality 4x5 negatives, so one would surmise that this was a professional working with a bellows camera.

New ALCO S3s on display, Windsor, 1956.

GARY NESS COLLECTION

This image offers a broad perspective on Water Street in Windsor and thus provides one of the more complete views of the alignment of the track through the town's business district.

Looking at these new diesel-electric locomotives, most people would have concluded that diesels were a recent development, but that would not have been true. The technology behind the diesel engine was quite old, dating back to the late 1800s when the diesel internal combustion engine was being developed by a number of inventors. Rudolf Diesel was ultimately credited with a major innovation in design, and the engine bears his name. In the early 1900s, he joined a collaborative that planned to manufacture direct-drive

diesel-powered locomotives, but the group had limited success.

Thomas Edison developed an early electric railcar, and General Electric (GE) developed a prototype for an electric locomotive, also around the turn of the century. Both worked but electricity was too expensive to make either one practical. Then Hermann Lemp, a brilliant GE electrical engineer, adapted the diesel engine to generate electricity to drive an electric motor that turned the axle on which wheels were mounted. His ideas lead to the building of three experimental diesel-electric locomotives in 1918.

New Dayliner No. 9058 on tour,
the Clementsport bridge, 1956.
LOUIS COMEAU / CP PHOTOGRAPHIC SERVICES

The two Dayliners' arrivals in August 1956 gained considerable attention, in part because of the CPR's efforts to promote the new modern approach. The railway hired a number of photographers to take publicity shots and to document the inauguration of the new service. The CP Photographic Services collection contains various builders' photographs showing the first Budd-built DAR Dayliner No. 9058 as it rolled out of the Red Lion Plant in Philadelphia, Pennsylvania. Also various views of No. 9058 were taken in the Glen yard in Montreal immediately after delivery, but some of the most appealing shots of No. 9058 were posed at a number of sites along the DAR. In particular, there are some very nice prints showing No. 9058 on the DAR's largest bridges, including those at Bear River and Clementsport (this page). One new Dayliner was sent on a promotional trip along the railway, stopping at numerous stations for extended periods while the public toured the car. Estimates indicate that over eleven thousand people inspected the car during these displays. Evidence suggests that the railway went to considerable lengths to make this tour successful.

New Dayliner on display at Windsor, August 1956.
LOUIS COMEAU / CP PHOTOGRAPHIC SERVICES

In the scene above at Windsor, Dayliner No. 9058 had entrance and exit signs posted over the doors at opposite ends of the car.

This was a classic shot of the DAR in transition from steam to diesel. No. 2551, one of the CPR's venerable G2s Pacifics, stood for a short time on the next track. This locomotive was one of the first CPR 4-6-2s to arrive on the DAR. Built in 1909 and sold to the DAR in 1940, this locomotive was scrapped in December 1959, after nineteen years as a DAR workhorse.

Steam locomotives of a given class may have a tendency to look similar, but in many ways they were unique, unlike diesels, which tend to be fairly uniform in appearance and performance. Retired engine men have often commented about the individual characteristics of steam locomotive performance and had preferences for some engines over others. The G2 Pacifics were a fine example of this variability.

For instance, many carried Elesco feedwater heater bundles in front of the smokestack while others had none. No. 2551 represents the latter and No. 2617 (pages 94 and 98) had a feedwater heater bundle.

Other variations, such as the three types of linkages for the reversing mechanism, were less prominent. No. 2551 had the most common type: a screw reverse system. Part of it can be seen extending forward out of the engineer's side of the cab and running diagonally downward along the boiler to about the midpoint, where it connects through the running board to the Walshaerts valve gear. This operated the upper piston valve, controlling the admission of steam to the main piston, which in turn provided thrust to the drivers. Inspection of other right-side views of G2 Pacifics does not reveal the screw reverse connection rod if a Johnson bar or air reverse type of linkage was installed.

DAR G2 No. 2516, Governor General's train, Digby, 1956.
ROBERT SANDUSKY

The DAR operated a number of regal and vice-regal special trains from August 1860 during a visit by the Prince of Wales. The train shown above was not a royal train, but Pacific No. 2516 was in the spotlight on June 28, 1956, when it was photographed at Digby with a special train for the Queen's representative, the Governor General of Canada, the Right Honourable Vincent Massey. No. 2516 was described by Omer Lavallée as "resplendent" in its fresh paint; one can see that it was gleaming.

The consist included a Canadian National Railway (CNR) green, yellow, and black battery-charging car No. 15200, formerly a Grand Trunk Railway (GTR) business car, and Canadian Pacific Railway (CPR) coaches plus heavy-weight business cars at the rear of the train. These last cars were the property of the Government of Canada.

The train stopped overnight in Kentville, where His Excellency may have stayed at the DAR's Cornwallis Inn.

When the train arrived in Kentville, No. 2516 was cut off the train and delivered to the roundhouse for servicing while Pacific No. 2551 moved the consist from in front of the station to the coach track.

The train continued westward the next day visiting various points along the Annapolis Valley route, including stops at Digby and Yarmouth. While in Digby, one of the DAR fast passenger trains arrived; the old CPR fruit car, just visible in the background of this photograph, was part of Train 95. It was in the process of being backed out to the pier by D10 No. 1077 to connect with the ferry *Princess Helene.*

Landlocked.

The DAR was landlocked, with its only access to the rest of Canada via the CNR at Truro and Halifax. That meant that the shortest transfer of locomotives to and from the nearest CPR terminal at Saint John, New Brunswick, was via the CNR's Springhill Subdivision (Truro–Moncton) and CNR's Sussex Subdivision (Moncton–Saint John).

Transfer of steam locomotives posed several problems if they were not working. For example, the movement of the pistons relied on internal steam pressures of 250 psi. When the locomotive was cold, the piston could not move with air trapped inside both the valve and the cylinder of the locomotive. The solution was to remove the drive rods (seen here on the walkway), which then allowed the drive wheels to turn freely. However, this created another problem. The heavy steel side rods that connected all drive wheels as a unit, moved in a circular motion, on the drive wheels. When the wheels were turning in that

circle, part of the motion was upward and downward, producing great pounding forces on the rails. To compensate, the drive wheels had counterbalances built into them directly opposite the points where the drive rods connected. These were the semicircular solid parts of the drive wheels. When all the rods, including the drive rods, were in place and rising, the counter weights were falling, and ideally this kept the drive rotating smoothly. The removal of the drive rod upset this balance.

D10 No. 1020 was at Truro in 1956, either coming from or going to Saint John. The drive rods were off. Their removal meant the drivers were unbalanced and would bounce and pound, so the CN freights that dragged No. 1020 to and from Saint John would have proceeded more slowly to reduce that effect on the wheels and track.

New hi-rail inspection station wagon.
HAROLD BAILEY

Inspection car M-107 (page 92) was replaced in 1957 by this hi-rail or road-rail vehicle, a new 1958 Pontiac station wagon. Posing with the new car, from left to right, are Doug Thoms (assistant engineer), J. C. McCuaig (DAR manager), Stan Gaudet (building and bridge master), and Don Hiltz (engineer).

The vehicle shown here was fairly typical in its use of hi-rail technology. The retractable, flanged wheels took approximately 40 per cent of the car's weight when in use; the vehicle's regular tires bore the remaining 60 per cent and provided motive and braking power when riding on the rails. The development of this technology resulted from the need to have greater economy and flexibility in railway inspection and maintenance of way vehicles. Hi-rail vehicles presented the railways with the ultimate in versatility. Unlike the highly modified M-107 superintendent's car that was confined to the rails, hi-railers could be driven on the highway or on access roads along the line. With clearance from the dispatcher, any convenient level crossing provided access to the rails. The driver aligned the tires and dropped the guide wheels. Transition back to the roadway was as simple and required only minutes to complete. Hi-rail vehicles also provided greater flexibility in rail traffic control; when the M-107 had to pass other trains, a siding was required and operators had to plan its movements like those of a regular train. On the other hand, hi-railers could leave the tracks at any number of sites.

DAR diesels and Dayliners; RDC 9058 on Bear River bridge, 1956.
LOUIS COMEAU / CP PHOTOGRAPHIC SERVICES

The DAR diesels and Dayliner era began with the transition from steam to diesel in 1956. In mid-August of that year, passenger service changed over to two Dayliners, Nos. 9058 and 9059. Both were labelled Dominion Atlantic. These were Budd-built RDC1s (Rail Diesel Cars). From that point, two RDC1s were always on the line until VIA took over. These included CPR/CP Rail RDC1 Nos. 9049, 9050, 9057, 9060, 9062, 9064, 9067, and 9072.

Two ALCO S3 diesel-electrics (Nos. 6560 and 6561) also arrived in 1956 for duty on gypsum trains. The S3s were equipped with multiple-unit (MU) cables that allowed them to be driven as one coupled unit; this was unique to these DAR S3s. Also unique was the fact that both the S3s and Dayliners arrived lettered "Dominion Atlantic."

Replacement of the S3s and most of the remaining steam locomotives occurred in 1959 when ten SW1200rs road switcher diesels,

Nos. 8131 to 8140, arrived. These were the core freight motive power until 1994. They, too, were equipped with MU cables. Two of these units, Nos. 8139 and 8140, were not needed and were returned after a trial period. Thereafter, some of the remaining eight were on the DAR for many years. By 1994 only four road switchers were required.

In 1980 CP Rail (the new name adopted by the CPR in 1968) began rebuilding and renumbering SW1200rs road switchers: Nos. 1271 (formerly No. 8125); 1272 (formerly No. 8116); 1273 (formerly No. 8143); 1274 (formerly No. 8126); 1275 (formerly No. 8130); and 1276 (formerly No. 8108) served on the DAR. Lastly, three rebuilt CP Rail RS18s, Nos. 1806, 1815, and 1824, did summer work on the DAR in the mid-1980s.

DAR Dayliner 9059 in the Halifax Cut, 1958.

It was April 19, 1958, and DAR Dayliner No. 9059 was on the first leg of its journey westbound as Train 11 from Halifax to Yarmouth. No. 9059 was exercising its running rights over CNR tracks and was on schedule, still on CNR tracks approximately two miles west of the Halifax passenger terminal, moving away from the photographer (hence no headlight showing in this image) and was about to pass under the Jubilee Road bridge. The second, more distant bridge was the Quinpool Road overpass.

Although passenger service between Yarmouth and Halifax was more rapid following the 1956 transition from steam trains to Dayliner service, patronage of the service continued to decline. The original Dayliner schedule had two Trains, 11 and 13, westbound daily-except-Sunday and Trains 12 and 14 eastbound; however, service was down to one Dayliner in each direction by the mid-1960s. In 1969 and 1977, CP applied to the Canadian Transportation Commission (CTC) to discontinue the service due to unprofitability. Public reactions, citing bad timetables and poor promotion of the service by CP, caused CP's application to fail. Undaunted, CP reapplied for abandonment in 1979. This, too, failed, but CTC ordered CP and the newly formed 1978 VIA Rail to upgrade services on the line for a one-year experimental period. The experiment worked and the improved VIA service lasted until 1989.

No. 1038 enters the roundhouse.
IAN DONALDSON

D10 No. 1038 appears to be ready for winter; the shop crew had hung the winterization curtains in the entryway between the locomotive and tender. During winter snowplow service a tarpaulin would also be used to cover the coal bunker. The draughty, open cab of No. 1038 is readily visible and contrasts with the enclosed cabs common on most of the Pacifics. Images on pages 113 and 95 offer excellent views of these features on both the G1 and G2 versions of CPR's 4-6-2 types. While the open cab may have been somewhat cooler in summer, it was uncomfortably cold in winter. The G1s and G2s were not built with enclosed all-weather or vestibule cabs. The Pacifics were rebuilt gradually and this common feature was included after it became the norm on more modern Canadian steam engines.

In spite of the drawbacks, it has been argued the D10s were an extremely successful design. Omer Lavallée has written that they were intended to be versatile and adaptable to diverse applications. Their success in meeting that objective was demonstrated by their ubiquity in Canadian rail photography. They were the largest class of steam engines in Canada, and the 502 locomotives of this class have been recorded on film in every corner of the CPR's extensive network. Their assignments included passenger, freight, mixed, and work trains and they even served as switchers in yard service. Regardless of assignment, they were considered real workhorses, capable of pulling considerable tonnage.

No. 2209 at Yarmouth, late 1950s.

One-of-a-kind on the DAR, G1s Pacific No. 2209 was waiting on the ready track in Yarmouth for the trainman, at the right rear of this photo, to throw the switch allowing the locomotive to back onto its train, which occupied the main line in front of the old freight shed at the right. Use of steam engines on scheduled passenger trains was officially over by the time this scene was photographed; yet the trainman is in his conductor's uniform, indicating it is likely this photograph captured one of those instances when there were too many passengers for a single Dayliner to carry. The two Dayliners were then coupled and a steam-drawn train of coaches made the opposing run. In this case, the train leaving Yarmouth was likely Train 11.

(CONTINUED NEXT PAGE)

G1 No. 2209 at Yarmouth, late 1950s.
GARY NESS COLLECTION

These photographs, both at Yarmouth, were undated; however, No. 2209 was one of the last four CPR steam locomotives to be sold to the DAR, and unlike many earlier locomotive transfers, these four locomotives were known from photographic evidence to have arrived at the time they were sold. No. 2209 and Ten-wheeler 1027 arrived here in November 1957 while Pacifics Nos. 2629 and 2501 arrived in March and July of 1958, respectively.

The photographs shown here were taken between November 1957 and February 1961, when 2209 was scrapped.

No. 1046 taking on coal and sand, Kentville, 1958.
IAN DONALDSON

When this September 1958 photo was taken of D10 No. 1046 backing to the sanding and coaling facilities in Kentville, none would have foreseen the cement superstructure of the coaling tower standing for over three decades as a reminder of the operations of steam locomotives on the DAR. Anyone familiar with the Kentville skyline during the 1960s, 1970s, and 1980s most certainly will recall that enduring hulk of the coaling tower standing like an implacable giant in the centre of the rail yards (page 137). It was finally demolished in the fall of 1990, but it did not yield easily. Built in the early 1940s, it was reinforced with steel rails in the vertical supports

The operation of the coaling tower was fairly simple. The hopper car sitting on the raised track under the tower dropped its coal load into a bunker beneath the track. An enclosed conveyer system lifted the coal to the bunker. The conveyer was housed in the tall structure on the back of the tower, which can be seen emerging upward just to the right of the hopper car. Coal was delivered into the tender coal bunker by pulling the rope on the delivery chute, visible at the lower left of the tower.

The wooden structure seen above No. 1046's tender was the sand tower. Fine sand was heated to dry it thoroughly, then stored in this bunker. The servicing of all steam locomotives also required that their sand dome be filled.

Preparing steam locomotives for the road, Kentville, late 1950s.
IAN DONALDSON

Photographers in years past tended to focus on trains in settings and situations that were quite predictable, such as station areas, pulling trains, and so on. This was partly due to the fact that film speeds were "slow" and could not capture a moving train; the trains had to be standing still or nearly so. Thus, at one time the most common type of train still photograph was the roster shot, which was just that: a photograph usually taken at a three-quarter angle to the front and slightly to the side in order to record the best close-up view of a single locomotive, often without a train. These much sought after images are still very collectable, much like sport cards.

However, a book featuring roster shots is also a little boring because it misses so much that is interesting about railways. It has always been fun to come across shots that reveal more about the surroundings or about the generally ignored aspects of everyday railway activities, such as the preparation of a steam engine for the road.

The workman crouching on the handrail beside the sand dome atop No. 1046's boiler was playing it safe as the hosteller eased the locomotive forward to the sand tower after filling No. 1046's coal bunker. The top of the coal load is just visible above the locomotive's cab.

Preparing steamers for the road, Kentville, late 1950s.
IAN DONALDSON

No. 1046 had inched forward to the sand tower in this late 1950s scene at Kentville. The fellow atop the boiler removed the watertight cover on the sand dome and was filling the sand dome with dry sand that the engineer would later use to sand the track.

Every steam locomotive had a sand dome with its attached delivery pipes extending down the sides of the locomotive and ending in line with and in front of the front driver. While the lower end of the sanding delivery pipe is not visible in this image, one can see it in front of the lead driver at truck level on page 105.

The engineer sanded the track when starting a heavy train or climbing hills to prevent wheel slip from loss of traction, which occurred on wet track or when the throttle application was just too much. When the drivers spun, the engineer had to back off the throttle quickly and then notch it up again. The notches were in the throttle mechanism with notch 8 being the highest power. The firemen, whose job was to maintain a hot fire by distributing coal evenly over the grate in the firebox, did not like it when the drivers slipped. The sudden vigorous use of steam in the pistons and its subsequent ejection up the stack pulled air violently through the fire from the grate and tore the fire apart. It also sucked smaller pieces of coal up the stack, which is why egg-sized coal was used.

The coal crane loading coal, Kentville, 1958.

Al Lockwood was operating the coal crane on August 30, 1958, at the coal yard near the back of the Kentville yards. He was the usual operator and in this case was loading the coal hoppers at the left for distribution to points on the DAR that needed coal. The end of steam was imminent and the coal pile in this scene is visibly low; before diesels, estimates suggest the reserve of coal here topped fifteen feet in height.

The coal crane was steam operated with a small boiler that was fired by periodically throwing in a few shovelfuls of coal. The cab could rotate 360 degrees and the clamshell scoop was very useful for other work around the yard.

The ash pit, where the cinders from steamers were dumped, was nearby. It needed periodic cleanup, and Al would take the crane there and load these same hoppers with cinders for disposal. Most often, the cinders were mixed with sand and gravel; the mix made high-quality, porous ballast that was spread along the right-of-way.

In the background, the roundhouse is apparent to the west and behind the coal piles to the right is the water tower, which was near the turntable.

The Cornwallis River is behind the coal yard and runs roughly parallel to the track in this scene.

*No. 2501
Mixed Train 2,
Truro, 1958.*
KEN MACDONALD

Scheduled Truro–Windsor Mixed Train 2, driven by John Warden and fired by Cyril White (visible in the window), had just left the CNR station in Truro at 8:30 AM on a sunny November 28, 1958. The train was seen ten minutes later, having just left the CNR main line tracks at the right. It had entered the Truro Subdivision of the DAR and was already stopped to carry out some switching duties. It would continue along the line in a rather leisurely fashion, exchanging passengers and switching freight cars at many points, and finally arrive in Windsor at 11:00 AM.

Railwaymen of the 1950s recall that it was uncommon for a Pacific, such as No. 2501, to pull this train. Usually D10s maintained

this service because of weight restrictions on bridges. In fact, when D10s first arrived on the DAR in the late 1930s and early 1940s, even they were deemed too heavy for the bridges. When a high-tonnage train required double-heading, fifteen cars would be placed between locomotives in order to reduce loading at bridges. Ironically, the Truro Subdivision was very busy, particularly just after World War Two when D10s were double-headed regularly and extra trains were frequently called for. Members of the Humphrey Club for retired DAR employees recall one train of that time with one hundred freight cars drawn by two D10s.

No. 2629 with Dayliner, Yarmouth, late 1950s.

Pacific No. 2629 and this train were occupying the main line in Yarmouth sometime between 1958, when the locomotive arrived on the DAR, and 1961, when the locomotive was scrapped. The sequence of a baggage car, a Dayliner, a coach, another baggage car, and finally another coach is strange. Trainmen of that time could not explain it; we discussed and rejected various ideas.

In the years 1958 to 1961, the two Dayliners provided passenger service in both directions along the Halifax–Yarmouth route. In exceptionally busy times, the two Dayliners would be coupled and a steam-drawn conventional passenger train would run. A diesel road switcher could not pull these conventional trains because it could not heat the train in the winter. In this photo the trainman is lightly dressed in short sleeves and it appears to be summer, but during the busy summer season the road switchers would be busy with other freight and work duties.

Unless the Dayliner had failed, it would not deadhead back to Kentville in a passenger train drawn by steam. Nobody recalled such an event.

The only explanation that made sense is the possibility that this was a switching move. Although one wonders why the Dayliner was not moving under its own power and why it was in the middle of a train.

SW1200rs diesels arrival, Kentville, 1959.
HAROLD BAILEY

In 1957 CPR committed to system-wide replacement of steam with diesel motive power by 1960. Thus, in 1959 ten SW1200rs diesel-electric units were delivered to the DAR. These units retired most DAR steam engines and replaced the two MLW S3 diesels that were too light for gypsum train service. The ten new diesels arrived over several weeks. The first units were placed in service on the last Monday of April 1959. Diesels Nos. 8131 and 8132 were parked near the Kentville shops prior to their first trip on the DAR, and DAR manager J. C. McCuaig was on the ground, apparently issuing instructions to Bob Copeland in the cab of No. 8131.

The SW1200rs locomotives were intended to operate as single units with the cab to the rear, although they are frequently seen running cab forward, or as multiple units with the cabs back to back as in this photograph. Multiple units (MU) could be controlled from one cab by one engineer by linking the units with MU cables between the diesels. In this image, the front MU cables have not yet been affixed to No. 8131, but the fitting for the cables are clearly visible to either side of the front coupler.

Hockey special, Kentville, c. 1959.
HAROLD BAILEY

Former DAR trainmen offered some completely different explanations for this diesel/steam double-header at Kentville.

It might have been a December 1959 passenger extra about to head westbound to Yarmouth with heavy Christmas traffic. Normally the two Dayliners operated as single units, but during periods of heavy traffic they were coupled and conventional equipment was used for the opposing train. No. 2209 was the only steam locomotive remaining on the DAR and had been retained to provide steam to heat the conventional coaches since No. 8131 was not equipped with a steam generator.

Alternatively, it also could have been a March 1960 hockey special provided to carry students from Kings County Academy in Kentville to Halifax for the annual hockey game with Queen Elizabeth High School students.

In fact it was a hockey extra associated with the Bruce Knight Series between Kentville's Kings County Academy (KCA) and Halifax's Queen Elizabeth High School (QEH). The train ran to Halifax where it picked up the team and students from QEH at the CNR Ocean Terminal. The students were delivered to the Kentville station in time for the late afternoon game and an early evening dance. The DAR then returned the QEH students to Halifax. These special hockey trains ran for years.

The two firemen, Harley H. MacLeod in No. 2209 and Rupert Parker in No. 8131, view the proceedings from above while other crew members, (from left to right) Arnold Mahoney, Earl Haines, Jake Corbin, and Jack Bishop, pose on the ground.

CHAPTER 6

THE DAR/CPR ERA: DAYLINERS AND ROAD SWITCHER DIESELS 1960–1994

◀ *Telltale danger, Annapolis Royal, 1962.* JIM SHAUGHNESSY

THIS SCENE FROM THE OLD RAILWAY BRIDGE AT ANNAPOLIS ROYAL WAS RECORDED IN 1962. IT REVEALS a telltale: the white upright timber structure at the right with ropes dangling from the armature, which was intended to warn brakemen of the approach of the low bridge. If you have not guessed by now, the telltale was a warning to brakemen to duck; the low bridge from which this image was shot would be just ahead. The telltale was a carry-over from the earliest days of train operations before the advent of modern brake systems.

Modern brake systems are controlled by pressurized air supplied by the locomotive via an interconnected, high-pressure brake-line under the cars. There is also a brake-wheel activated mechanism for locking standing cars in place.

In the pioneer days, there was no brake-line extending the length of the train. Instead, each car was equipped with its own stem-winder brake-wheel, which was tightened or released by hand to control the momentum of that car. The stem-winder wheels were most prominent on the roofs of boxcars. A stem-winder brake can be seen projecting above the boxcar on page 26. If sufficient braking were applied to the correct cars, train speed and slack in the train could be controlled; however, bringing a train to a controlled stop or controlling its speed down a hill required considerable judgment if the links were to stay seated on the pins. For brakemen on the cars during sudden or emergency stops or derailments, it must have been a nightmare. Operating on dark nights or in heavy rain or snow was also dangerous.

SW1200rs
No. 8134
passing
Grand-Pré
Park, 1962.
JIM SHAUGHNESSY

The introduction of diesels in the colourful new paint schemes attracted substantial interest in the 1950s; however, the demise of steam, coupled with the loss of the diesels' novelty, led to a decline in interest for DAR photography that endured throughout the 1960s. Compared to other decades, it has been difficult to find shots of the DAR SW1200rs units in their original paint schemes during the 1960s. It was fortuitous that Jim Shaughnessy, a noted railway photographer and contributor to many publications about railways, visited Nova Scotia in 1962 and on July 13 and 14 took this and other excellent photographs. In this scene, Nos. 8134 and 8133 were passing Grand-Pré with what appears to be a scheduled eastbound run, probably either Train 26 or 50, the daily-except-Sunday second- and fourth-class freights, respectively.

The DAR, like the CPR, recognized the value and potential of tourism and became an early leader in that industry in the Valley. The CPR had been credited with the initiation of our national park system after Banff was created; the DAR had a similar effect in Nova Scotia. At the right of this scene is the Grand-Pré National Historic Site, one of the sites of the Acadians' deportation by the British. In 1908 legislation safeguarded the property as an historically important area, but it was not until the DAR purchased it in 1916 and developed the park and its historic displays that it became a major attraction and historical monument.

Princess Helene *arriving, Saint John, New Brunswick, 1963.*
GARY NESS COLLECTION

The SS *Princess Helene* was built in 1930 in Dunbarton, Scotland, by Denny Shipyard. When this 1963 photograph was taken in Saint John, the vessel was thirty-three years old and in her last year of service on the route. The SS *Princess of Acadia* would soon replace it on the Digby–Saint John run.

The *Princess Helene* had taken over from the SS *Empress*, an older, smaller ship built in 1916. Often referred to as "the Digby boat," the *Princess Helene* was built for this particular CPR service as part of the CPR Short Line between Halifax and Montreal and thus was considered an extension of renowned CPR first-class service. The ferry was outfitted for class and charm like the typical and much larger transatlantic Duchess liners of the time. Its forty-three staterooms were reputed to be quite tastefully appointed and of a standard well above other Canadian ferries at the time.

At 4,000 tons, 320 feet long, and with a beam of 51 feet, *Princess Helene* was well designed for stability in the frequently rough Bay of Fundy. It could carry five hundred passengers, fifty automobiles, and tons of freight by way of the side-loading doors. Elevators on the wharfs were designed to deal with tidal changes in the bay (page 70). In all, the Digby boat steamed 168,400 miles during thirty-three years of service, including World War Two when it was often escorted by warships and anti-submarine aircraft because of German U-boats.

One might wonder why an image of a CNR diesel appears in a book about the DAR. In fact, the diesel was on the DAR main line in Middleton at the point where the CNR's Middleton Subdivision crossed the DAR tracks at grade level—by way of two switches that served as the crossover. The CNR trains would be on the DAR very briefly before returning to CNR tracks and the forty-mile trip to their port facilities at Port Wade on the Annapolis Basin.

The CNR line across the middle of the province from Bridgewater Junction on the CNR Chester Subdivision included the former Nova Scotia Central Railway (NSCR) and the Middleton and Victoria Beach Railway (M&VBR). The latter extended beyond the DAR crossing at Middleton to Torbrook and Port Wade, although the CNR timetable referred to the northern end point as Bridgetown.

The NSCR line between Middleton in the Annapolis Valley and Bridgewater on the South Shore was opened on December 23, 1889. The incomplete M&VBR was sold to the Halifax and South Western Railway (H&SWR) in 1905, after which the line was completed. By the early 1980s CN had decided that the South Shore line and the Middleton Subdivision were not going to regain their profitability for freight or passenger services and applied to abandon all of it. The abandonment of the CN's South Shore line beyond Liverpool and the Middleton Subdivision was granted in 1982.

Dayliner/Burro crane wreck, Kentville, 1965.
HAROLD BAILEY

During the 1960s and 1970s DAR passenger traffic had declined to the point at which single Dayliners were more than adequate for most situations; however, both Dayliners travelled to Yarmouth every Friday evening. Since Train 4, the scheduled Saturday-only morning passenger run from Kentville to Halifax, required one of the self-propelled units, a single Dayliner would leave Yarmouth as Train 8 at 2:30 AM and run back to Kentville in the dark. Unfortunately on October 31, 1965, someone forgot No. 8 was inbound, and the Burro, with its accompanying boom flatcar, left Kentville westbound for Bridgetown too soon. The opposing trains had a cornfield meet at 7:32 AM about three miles west of Kentville.

The Dayliner engineer, Lloyd Ritchie, seeing that a collision was imminent, applied the emergency brakes, "put the Dayliner into emergency," opened the door to the passenger compartment and shouted a warning to those aboard. He was hurt badly and was hospitalized for a long period. Conductor Albert "Shine" Manning injured his neck, and he, too, went to hospital. However, thanks to Ritchie's prompt actions, the nine passengers who went to hospital were all treated for minor injuries and released.

The wreck was so tightly jammed together that it had to be hauled to Kentville to be separated. The Dayliner and Burro were sent to Montreal. While the Burro eventually returned to the DAR, Dayliner No. 9058—one of the original two assigned to the DAR (No. 9059 was the other)—was sent elsewhere after repair and never returned.

*Mixed
Train 21
en route,
Truro, 1967.*
BILL LINLEY

Small railways like the DAR were attractive destinations for train fans from around the world. Their continued use of smaller steam locomotives—built between 1905 and 1915—during the late 1950s and early 1960s was unusual because diesels had taken over on most main lines. Additionally, the DAR was a place to find other interesting holdouts and anachronisms. For example, the Windsor–Truro

mixed trains continued to run long after such practices were halted on nearly all other North American lines. For this reason, rail fans still visited the DAR into the 1970s.

In the mid-1960s, when these photos were taken of Train 21, the mixed daily-except-Sunday run, left Windsor at 4:00 PM on its 2.5-hour, 56.9-mile trip to Truro. It was due back in Windsor the next day.

Tracks on Water Street, Windsor, 1967.

BILL LINLEY

The pre-causeway track alignment in Windsor followed a large S-curve, travelling up the middle of Water Street in the town's core (page 103) then completing a sweeping curve towards the bridge spanning the Avon River estuary, shown on page 85. That fact was clear in the old photos, but many details in the background of those shots were obscured, too far away, or had changed over time. This more recent image filled in a lot of detail so that one can visualize the reality.

The original line, the Windsor Branch, was intended only to reach the Bay of Fundy to provide the most direct overland connection to shipping in the Bay of Fundy. The obvious approach to Windsor was along the east side of the hill on which Fort Edward stood. However, the subsequent building of the Windsor and Annapolis Railway needed to interchange goods and passengers with the Windsor Branch before heading west. There has been some conjecture that the W&AR wanted a more direct line through Windsor, but a cut through the large rise of land that forms the centre of the town would have been cost prohibitive. An additional factor may have been linked to the ongoing acrimony between the two lines. As mentioned (page 8), for several years after construction began on the Western Counties line, the rival lines exchanged passengers and freight across a platform rather than by direct movement of cars from one line to the next; the latter would be considered more normal and efficient!

Caboose No. 436617, crew quarters at Truro, February 16, 1969.

JIM O'DONNELL

The 56.9-mile runs of the daily-except-Sunday Windsor–Truro Mixed Trains 21 and 22 were not long trips; however, the April 1969 timetable called for Train 21 to depart Windsor at 1400 hours (2:00 PM) and arrive in Truro at 1630 hours (4:30 PM), while Train 22 departed Truro at 0700 hours (7:00 AM) and arrived in Windsor at 0930 hours (9:30 AM). Thus crews were required to overnight in Truro. Such ongoing crew accommodation could have been expensive, but wasn't. Besides needing a place to house the rear-end train crew as the train rolled towards its destination, there was also the need to accommodate crews at turnaround sites before they began their return trips. This was managed in some cases by having crew

quarters on railway property, as they did on the second floor of the Kentville station. In more out-of-the way locales, cabooses, such as No. 436617, could be parked on a quiet siding overnight or for longer periods. Vans outfitted for this purpose had bunks, very basic kitchens, washrooms, and stoves.

A decade later, during the final years of mixed train service on the Midland, both freight and passenger traffic had declined to the point that the train had no passengers, other than a few rail fans, and freight service was only marginally better; neither was making a profit. The train ran to Truro and returned on the same day and a layover was unnecessary.

Snowplow train, Annapolis Royal, Christmas 1970.
ROBERT TAYLOR / HAROLD BALSOR COLLECTION

Every winter in the Annapolis Valley, a few severe blizzards with high winds caused snow accumulation that required plow trains. Unfortunately, when others were at home enjoying the festive day with their families and friends, the train shown here was called for duty on Christmas Day, December 25, 1970, to clear the line between Annapolis Royal and Digby.

Plowing relied on the locomotive to ram the plow through drifts. If it bogged down, the train would back out and attempt again to ram through the snow mass. However, as the plow moved through a drift, the walls of snow to either side of the train collapsed into the trench behind it. Since the wooden cabooses of the era were far lighter than the heavily constructed steel-sheathed plows, a backing move led by the caboose could result in the caboose being lifted off the tracks. This scenario was not a typical derailment since the caboose's wheels would be buried under deep snow. Re-railing the car meant first digging down to expose the wheels. Then the heavy steel re-railer mechanism could be wrestled through the snow and into the hole.

In the case of the train in this photo, there were two versions of the story, both with supporters. One suggests that when the train was plowing out a cut west of Annapolis Royal where the accumulated snow was unexpectedly deep and when a backing move was required, the scenario described above occurred. The other version of the story was that the train derailed during a backing movement on the wye in Digby. Regardless of how it happened, this was a most unpleasant mishap for a crew on Christmas Day.

Workin' on the railroad, Wolfville, 1983.
GARY NESS

To the public, station masters and operating crews—engineers, firemen, conductors, and trainmen—were the most obvious railway employees, and to varying degrees they were romanticized by young boys. However the railways could not have functioned without a huge cohort of workers who quietly and proudly carried out their jobs. This DAR section gang was doing just that—workin' on the railroad—at Wolfville just east of the Victoria Lane extension that provides access to the Grand-Pré dykelands. The sign to their left indicates the level crossing just ahead.

This photograph shows the crew doing track work, including ditching, which was mostly accomplished by the Burro crane. Their shift was almost over; the crew had packed up for the day and was waiting for the Burro to complete its task. Although clearing ditches

and reshaping them to ensure good runoff flow might not seem very important and certainly not romantic, there were times when drainage really mattered. Spring thaws could overwhelm drainage if ditches were choked with weeds and debris. When water built up, before it could drain away it would overtop or run around the blockage, and erosion of the elevated roadbed could result. It was better to keep water moving slowly and under control.

The long, elevated piece of track curving away into the distance in both of these photographs was the length of track on the newly completed W&AR railway that was the most heavily damaged by the Saxby Gale, which struck on October 4/5, 1869. Water destroyed much of the newly built line between Wolfville and Hortonville.

Workin' on the railroad, Wolfville, 1983.
GARY NESS

The Saxby Gale had hurricane-force winds, which drove an immense volume of tidal water into the Minas Basin. The high tide, combined with huge waves, overwhelmed the dykes and washed them away. They are not visible in these photographs, but the flat expanse of land to the left of the track is dyked farm fields, which, were it not for the dykes, would be under water during high tides. The failure of the dykes in 1869 allowed the sea to reach the tracks and overflow the roadbed as well.

The 1869 storm lasted for days. The turbulent high tides and waves washed away a lot of the fill under the tracks, and the runoff afterwards took even more away. Nearly twenty miles of bridges and tracks were damaged. In places, tracks with ties still attached hung in the air.

When the storm was over, Vernon Smith immediately put repair crews to work. By mid-November the line was nearly ready for use. A subsequent high tide swept over the railway, undoing much of their work. By the first of December, when the next really high tide would occur, hasty repairs had been done. The tide again topped the railway, leaving more damage in its wake. After that, an expected period of lower tides held, and repairs were completed. This time they remained.

*Caboose
No. 437293,
Wolfville,
1983.*

GARY NESS

CP Rail caboose No. 437293 was serving a stint on the DAR in this April 28, 1983, photo at Wolfville. Work Extra 8136 had arrived in Wolfville with a ballast train ahead of the scheduled VIA Dayliner, Train 152 from Yarmouth to Halifax. The ballast train took the siding to give way to the passenger train. VIA RDC 8122 (Rail Diesel Car was another term for Dayliners) and an unidentified second RDC arrived on time and departed eastbound at 10:45 AM, after which the work train, comprising road switcher 8136 and four loaded ballast cars, uncoupled from the caboose and proceeded eastbound spreading ballast along the track just west of Grand-Pré.

The conductor, Fred Wilcox, stayed with the caboose and promptly set about spring housecleaning, which lasted for some time before the ballast train returned. The locomotive then ran around the ballast cars using the siding before putting the caboose back on the rear of the train, which then faced westbound for the return trip to the quarry for more ballast loads.

At that time, caboose No. 437293 would have been described as a CP Rail standard, modern, steel, offset cupola type. It was painted in the action yellow scheme.

Visiting RS18 No. 1806, Wolfville, 1985.
GARY NESS

In 1981 CP Rail initiated a major upgrading and rebuilding of many of its first-generation diesels rather than purchase expensive new models. CP's RS18 road switcher diesels (Nos. 8729 to 8800 in CP classes DRS18a and b) were chosen for continued service as road switchers and refurbished with a chopped short hood, new electrical systems, an improved cab interior design, and were renumbered in the 1800s.

RS18s did not appear on the DAR prior to the rebuilding program. However, No. 1806, rebuilt from No. 8748, was seen on April 15, 1985, eastbound at Wolfville on the head end of a ten-car ballast train, making the first run of any RS18 over DAR tracks. It had arrived on the DAR, dead-in-tow, the previous evening. Its engine

was started in the Kentville shop early on the following morning and it hauled the empty ballast cars to the Round Hill pit four miles east of Annapolis Royal, where it was loaded. It then proceeded eastbound, passing Wolfville at 11:30 AM.

Fully loaded, ten-car ballast trains were too heavy for a single SW1200rs, and No. 1806 was assigned to the DAR to avoid tying up two SW1200rs units with summer track ballasting work; by 1985 a total of only five SW1200rs diesels were assigned to the DAR. No. 1806 remained on the DAR for the summer months, completing ballast work at various points across the system, before returning to the CP in August 1985. Another RS18 No. 1815 was assigned to similar work on the DAR from October 21 to November 23, 1985.

Fundy Gypsum Company GE switcher, Hantsport, 1985.

GARY NESS

It was March 1985 at Hantsport and SW1200rs Nos. 8133 and 8132, in the background with the caboose, had just arrived with a gypsum train from Dimock's. Fundy Gypsum Company's forty-five-ton General Electric industrial switcher, No. 646, had backed out of the company's track to the right and would take the cars, six at a time, through the unloading facility. The gypsum was loaded onto ships for transport to manufacturing facilities in the United States.

At that time, Fundy Gypsum operated five General Electric switchers: No. 647, another forty-five-tonner, served at the Miller's Creek Quarry. Two twenty-five-tonners, Nos. 640 and 641, served at Wentworth quarry, and No. 642, a third twenty-five-tonner, worked at the Miller's Creek facility.

Apple Blossom Festival Special, Kentville, 1986.
GARY NESS

The DAR found many ways to be engaged in its local communities. Their annual involvement in the Apple Blossom Festival was a prime example. In this 1986 scene, Train 152 was the scheduled train from Yarmouth. In this case, three cars went to Yarmouth on the previous evening so that the train could pick up dignitaries and family members along the Valley en route to Kentville. At Kentville, there were approximately two hundred people on it.

The crew for this train included engineer Floyd Russell, conductor R. D. (Doug) Jolly (both were the regular senior crew members on this run), plus trainmen Robert Arenburg and Peter Laing

who were added off the spare board because the rules required a trainman dressed in his conductor's uniform for each added car.

The train was slightly late due to stops to board all the passengers. It was greeted in Kentville by a platform filled with festival organizers, festival and Valley mascots, the royal party (Queen Annapolisa and the princesses), RCMP officers in their red serge, dignitaries from Kentville and from the eastern end of the Valley, plus numerous well-wishers. A band played on the flatcar at the left.

DAR crews remember these trains fondly and were pleased to be able to work on them.

Recollections: Driving the DAR Way Freight, Train 50 by Engineer Jim Murray.

A regular afternoon in the mid-1980s had a freight train from Kentville terminal at 15:15. After preparatory inspection of the engines, I receive a register check and train orders. Our engines leave the shops along the old Central Valley Railway (CVR) up to the main track of the Dominion Atlantic Railway (DAR).

Following a holiday that has backed the freight service up, there are many extra freight cars to be taken from Kentville to Halifax Ocean Terminal (HOT). The through siding and yard track north one are full, so a double over is made and the brake test completed. More length, more time; I recall Albert "Shine" Manning saying, "Time, tide and the DAR wait for no man." The railroad administration frowns upon long initial terminal time at the rail yard and wants the trains out of the terminal as quickly as possible and out on the road. Knowing the Dayliner from Halifax is about to leave the Halifax terminal, we are obliged to leave the train yard and make our own meet farther down the rail.

Leaving Kentville, I know that Port Williams has cars in its lower through siding and so the next choice that is clear is Horton Landing. However, we have more train length than the siding can hold. This means stopping clear of the east switch at Horton Landing, cutting off the train and running out the head-end brakeman to flag the Dayliner coming from Halifax. After about thirty minutes, the headlights of the passenger train can be seen in the distance and it is brought into the through siding. I pull the train ahead clearing the west switch with the caboose, and the Dayliner continues out of the siding and along to Port Williams where he meets the Dayliner from Yarmouth. Our rear-end brakeman flags the superior Dayliner from Yarmouth on the dyke just west of Grand-Pré and brings him into Horton Landing. This time I back the freight up and he leaves through the east switch towards Halifax, and twenty minutes later we follow.

At Windsor we register our train and proceed to Windsor Junction where we again register our train, unlock the CNR main track switch, press the block indicator to verify the track is unoccupied, open the switch and enter the Canadian National Railway main line.

Pulling out onto the continuous welded rail is different. I can feel the smooth track beneath the wheels and the quiet that is due to not crossing rail joints every thirty-nine feet. Soon, away from Windsor Junction and down by the Bedford rock quarry, a home owner, watering his garden, decides to wash our engines as we pass by and sprays water into the cab through the open window. We continue down the Bedford Subdivision grade, picking up speed through Rockingham and over the South-West Junction switch onto Armdale and into OT (Ocean Terminal).

After dropping the train, tying it down, changing operating ends in the locomotives, completing engine brake tests, running around to pick up loads and then completing another brake test on the train, we are ready to leave the yard.

Leaving the yard tracks requires checking two block indicators and opening three switches, allowing us to cross over to the west-bound track. Once away from OT, running under signal indication to Bedford, we are handed our train orders. At Windsor Junction, we pick up ten large UTLX tanks of aviation fuel for Greenwood and two propane tanks for Kentville and Digby. From there, we travel down the main line to the first crossover switch, check the block indicator, and proceed onto the eastbound track running against the current of traffic to the DAR main track switch and enter the DAR Halifax Sub.

Having left Windsor Junction and passed Newport Station crossing, the flats of Three Mile Plains are visible. Ahead I can see a person and a large dog standing beside the tracks. The person decides, for some reason, to change sides and cross the track with her dog. At this time we have blown for another crossing and the girl obviously felt uncomfortable on that side of the track, so she crossed over the tracks again. The dog, however, became confused so he sat in the middle of the tracks. Sadly we had no choice and continue down the track upset about the incident.

After we return to Kentville, the night yard train crew then takes over and switches out our train. They assemble Train 25 to Yarmouth, road switcher Train 1 and Train 50 back to Halifax, and complete any other local work that is required.

RECOLLECTIONS: DRIVING THE DAR MORNING GYPSUM TRAIN BY ENGINEER JIM MURRAY.

When the phone rings in most people's homes at 3:00 AM, it is usually an emergency of some sort. However, in a railroad family's home a 3:00 AM phone call is a two-hour call to be on duty. This morning there has been about an eight-inch snowfall and the temperature is about minus twelve Celsius. There are three units on the shop track and a caboose to pick up out of the van track. Finishing the walk-around, preparatory inspection, and being given a train register check by the head-end brakeman, we depart the shop track. I nose into the van track and couple onto a caboose and back out again on the old Central Valley Railway (CVR) Spur. We proceed to the switch onto the main line, which has already been opened by the rear-end brakeman; we pass the switch by several engine lengths to prepare for a drop-by.

Upon a signal from the brakeman, I reverse the engines, apply power and we start to roll, then touch-up the independent brake creating slack that allows the rear brakeman to uncouple the caboose from the engines. I release the independent brake, and the engines speed away from the van and clear the switch as the head-end brakeman throws the switch closed before the van fouls the points of the switch. As the van rolls down the main line, the rear-end brakeman applies the handbrake and stops the caboose in the clear on the main line. The front-end brakeman brings us out onto the main line and couples us to the caboose. From there we travel up to the station, receive a brake test from the car-man and our train orders from the train operator.

Once the conductor registers us out of Kentville, we are away into the snowy morning. After leaving Avonport and continuing down the hill to Blue Beach, I notice a light waving at us near the track. We stop and are told by the people waving us down that their cattle are on the track. We proceed slowly, passing the animals, and continue to Hantsport. At Hantsport we pick up thirty-two empty gypsum cars and perform a brake test. Now we continue to Windsor and onto the Truro Subdivision. We register in and check for arrival of the Mixed Train 22 from Truro. We will continue from here toward Mantua or Dimocks. On this day, the station agent indicates in a note that it will be two and a half trips out of Mantua.

Leaving Windsor and running along the St. Croix River at other times of the year, I often see the tidal bore running along the river floor. However, today the St. Croix River is filled with ice cakes moving along slowly with the approaching high tide. A coyote makes its way quickly across an open field as he hears the rumble of the train as we cross the St. Croix River bridge. An adult eagle sits cautiously in an old, tall tree farther down the river, watching for a meal.

Stopping at the Mantua gypsum quarry main track switch, the front-end brakeman climbs down and walks up to the switch. It needs to be swept out because of the new snowfall, otherwise the points of the switch may not be firmly positioned against the outside rail, and if this happens, as the engines pass over the points the wheels could drop on the ground. After the switch is swept, pulled, and finally turned, the derailer is opened and the brakeman gives a come-ahead signal to enter the yard.

While all this is happening on the head-end, the rear-end trainman is closing both brake-line angle cocks between the last empty gypsum car and the caboose itself. He bleeds off the air reservoir and allows the caboose to be pulled along until it arrives just north of the highway crossing. I then move the throttle to off, creating slack back to the caboose. The rear-end trainman then pulls the uncoupling lever and applies the handbrake so as to stop the caboose from fouling the first switch, which would prevent our return runaround with the locomotives.

With the caboose cut off and the empty gypsum cars hauled clear of the adjacent track, our head-end brakeman separates the engines from the cars and applies handbrakes, while I am changing operating ends; this involves going back to the third engine and setting it up for the controlling movement. After more switch cleaning, I then return to retrieve the caboose from the south end of the yard and bring it to the north end to be placed on the gypsum loads. A little harder coupling to the caboose—than they would have preferred—is caused by the deeper snow preventing the wheels from heating up against the brake shoes. This creates less heat friction in the independent brake on the engines. We then go back around with the locomotives to the south end, the brakeman couples us to our train and the locomotives start pumping air into the air lines of loaded cars to perform a number one brake test.

Approximately twelve minutes later I apply the automatic brake and the rear and front-end trainmen begin their inspection walk. At mid-train they signal for brake release, cross over the cars to the opposite side, and return to their front- and rear-end positions. A signal from the tail end tells me to start pulling ahead out of the yard toward the crossing. As I stop at the Mantua public highway crossing, a school bus filled with children looking out the windows at the approaching train continues over the track and on its way. Downhill from the crossing my next stop is the main line switch to enter the Truro Spur. Again the front-end brakeman trudges up to the switch, opens it, and with a signal, we come ahead.

Knowing the spot, next to a fence by that tree, tells me that the rear wheels of the caboose are just rolling over the switch and in a moment or two there is a highball signal and we are away. Along into Windsor, across the fields, and the St. Croix River bridge, the timetable states to watch out for rock slides at mile 2.2 of the Truro Sub. At Windsor it's register again and get the train order that reads: "Work Extra 8131 between Windsor and Hantsport not protecting against extra trains, and other 19Y orders."

After opening up the Truro Sub switch and dragging onto the Halifax Subdivision, another of my track-side markers, a guard rail on the causeway at Mile Post 32, tells me the caboose is approaching the switch and the rear brakeman returns the switch to the normal position, and with him back aboard and a highball signal, we are away. With 7 million pounds of contents and tare this is a light train by CP standards.

The steepest hill on the DAR is Shaw's Bog at 1.8 per cent grade. With the throttle in number notch 8, our train thunders through Falmouth and ascends the hill. A blow for Akins Crossing and the train is quickly slowing down as the engines are now about mid-hill. Sanders on, with little effect, white lights flash on the instrument panel indicating wheel slip and I reduce the throttle, but slip continues and the speedometer registers two miles per hour. With the continuous wheel slip causing rough and jerky slack action, I

walk out on the gangway and down the steps carrying the big yellow wrench. The sanders are plugged full and nothing is coming out so I hit the pipes to loosen the compacted snow, but this does nothing. By the time I have returned to the cab the brakeman has reset the yellow vigilant alarm button twice.

In the rear, the conductor is concerned regarding the roughness of the slack action on the train that could break a coupler knuckle, leaving the train in two separate sections. Also there is concern for the morning passenger train's time from Kentville that we are encroaching upon. Meanwhile, as the caboose slowly clears Akins Crossing the engines spin out and the train stalls so I apply the brakes. The forward trainman walks back about halfway and separates the train. With three engines and half the cars we are able to climb the rest of the hill to Shaw's Bog siding.

At the top, loads are left on the main line just clear of the east siding switch. The locomotives are brought back through the siding and returned to the remaining train. This section is brought up the hill and uncoupled prior to the east switch. The engines are then taken up through the siding and back down the main line, the sections are coupled and again we are ready to go. Leaving Shaw's Bog is no problem as it is downhill into Mount Denson and into Hantsport.

At Hantsport the section men have the switches cleared out, and as the front-end trainman dashes ahead and turns the switch we follow into Hantsport yard. Time is limited before the arrival of the Kentville Dayliner to Halifax and we stay at the west end of the yard, in the clear, to await its arrival. After the passenger train has gone, we come down to the station and our first trip is finished.

As the snow has now been pushed back by the train, the second trip runs more smoothly as we meet the road switcher, out of Kentville, working at Windsor yard. It has brought freight from Kentville and picked up cars along the way for the Truro way freight 21 from Windsor. At Windsor, the freight from Truro, Train 22, is taken by road switcher Train 1 (the morning yard) back to Kentville. On the third trip up to Hantsport we meet Train 50 from Kentville, and they take over the final two and a half trips out of Mantua.

We leave for Kentville with one engine and caboose. As I blow for the Port Williams crossing it is becoming dusk. Crossing signals *are activated, yet just at the leading edge of the crossing a dark object remains between the rails, so I place the brake valve in emergency position. It takes more distance to warm up the brakes to grab and the sanders to help stop the train, as we approach what looks like a ski jacket between the rails. As the engines grind the sand on the rails, we stop about four car lengths from the object. The front brakeman walks up to take a look and discovers it is a large, black garbage bag stuffed with a Christmas tree that had blown onto the tracks. Tired and stressed, I continue toward the Kentville terminal. Another forty-five minutes and our train is put away and our work day has drawn to an end.*

Earl Giles of Port Williams, a retired teacher and long-time rail fan, was watching intently as rebuilt SW1200rs No. 1275 carefully positioned VIA Dayliner No. 6229 on the old air-operated turntable in front of the Kentville roundhouse. This photograph, taken on a May evening in 1986, was a regular event at that time. The scheduled daily VIA train from Halifax to Yarmouth often consisted of two Dayliners as far as Kentville, where one was left overnight and returned to Halifax the next day on the scheduled morning train coming back from Yarmouth. The car left in Kentville was usually turned before its run back to Halifax. While the RDC (Dayliner) was self-propelled, it still required assistance to position it on the turntable, which was only eighteen inches longer than its wheelbase.

The old turntable acted like a teeter-totter: when the weight of the RDC's lead truck passed beyond the midpoint of the turntable, the end of the turntable nearest No. 1275 rose slightly. This required the second truck of the RDC to jump up onto the near edge of the turntable track—a difficult action to control when the leading wheels have only eighteen inches to spare before running off the far end.

No. 1275 not only provided braking power and fine control in positioning the Dayliner, but also subsequently backed away about five feet, coupled an air hose to the turntable's air line and provided air pressure to power the two cylinder, air-operated engine attached to the turntable side, just to the left of the Dayliner's rear wheels.

Caboose 437484 on freight, Windsor, 1988.

In July 1988 CP Rail caboose 437484 would have been considered modern. It was steel and featured a centre cupola, a look that was quite different from the CPR's long-lasting, wood offset cupola cabooses that had been around since the early 1900s.

The long use of cabooses was ending and caboose-less CP Rail main line trains would start in 1989. Prior to that, cabooses were critical to the railways for many reasons. They provided accommodations on the road; storage for personal items in lockers; an end-of-train place for a crew to perform chores such as switching; protection of the rear end when stopped; a desk for the conductor to do his paperwork; a stove for heating and cooking; as well as an elevated place to observe the train for load shifting, damaged equipment or cargo, smoke from overheating axles dragging equipment,

and rear-end braking if necessary. As cars became taller, wide-vision cupolas (page 159) allowed side views of the train.

Caboose-less operation occurred due to advances in detection and safety technology, including line-side defect detectors and hot box detectors, and the development of the flashing rear-end devices (FREDs) or end-of-train (EOT) devices that monitored brake air pressure at the end of the train and reported movement of the last car to the cab when starting a heavy train. The EOT also provided a blinking light at the end of the train.

Of course there was a financial inducement for the change as well; the crew would move to the cab and it could be smaller to accommodate just the conductor and engineer.

Gypsum train operations, Dimock's, 1988.
GARY NESS

This July 27, 1988, image offers some insight into the day-to-day operations of the gypsum unit trains, which constituted the major source of traffic on the DAR in later years. At that time, an average of 1.8 million tons of gypsum was shipped over the line annually.

Work Extra 1273, a loaded twenty-five-car train of gypsum led by SW1200rs No. 8134 with Nos. 1275 and 1273 following, was approaching the Fundy Gypsum Company's Wentworth quarry operation at Dimock's, Mile 2.3 of the Truro Spur. The train was westbound, returning from Mantua, Mile 4.4, where it dropped off twenty-five empties at the Miller's Creek facility and picked up the loaded cars.

The train originated at Hantsport earlier that morning with No. 1273 leading after it had received radio clearance from the Saint John dispatcher to operate between Hantsport and Mantua. Train orders were based on the lead unit's number prior to leaving Hantsport; the train remained as Work Extra 1273 for the rest of the operation, regardless of direction of travel or an apparent change in lead units. The crew—an engineer, conductor, and two brakemen—had to remember this; all radio communications referred to the three locomotives collectively as "1273," the lead engine. When the train was performing switching movements on this return trip, the engineer was given instructions to "go ahead" or "back up" based on the direction that unit No. 1273 was facing.

It's 1992, and although things look the same between the time that the preceding photo of a gypsum train was taken and this photo of westbound gypsum train Work Extra 1274 on the St. Croix River bridge, there had been really bad news for the DAR.

Declining revenues during the 1980s caused CP Rail to isolate the lines east of Montreal into a new business unit, the Canadian Atlantic Railway (CAR), in September 1988. This included the main line east of Megantic, Quebec, through Maine and New Brunswick to Saint John, and all the associated branch lines, as well as the DAR. The headquarters of the new company was Saint John, New Brunswick.

While CP Rail issued public relations statements that the new company would have a better opportunity to improve its financial performance in the new model, most observers knew this was the beginning of the end for these operations as a component of CP Rail, which was focused on its heavy-haul main lines.

When the CAR was created, the DAR included the Halifax Subdivision (Kentville to Windsor Junction); the Kentville Spur (4.6 miles west from Kentville to the end of track at Coldbrook); the Kingsport Spur (2.3 miles north from Kentville to the end of track at the Ralston-Purina plant in Centreville); the Truro Spur (4.4 miles east from Windsor to the Fundy Gypsum Spur); and the Fundy Gypsum Spur (0.7 miles from the end of the Truro Spur to the gypsum plant at Miller's Creek).

These lines and especially the bridges were in disrepair; permanent speed restrictions were as little as thirty or ten miles per hour in places. Abandonments and service cuts continued during the CAR era from 1988 to 1994.

Gypsum train alongside the St. Croix River, August 1992.

A. ROSS HARRISON

In this photograph westbound gypsum train Work Extra 1274 approaches the Fundy Gypsum at Dimock's (Wentworth) along the St. Croix River. This elevated picture was taken in August 1992 atop a large gypsum outcropping that created a wonderful vantage point for photographers.

Co-op Atlantic grain traffic, New Minas, 1990.
GARY NESS

Work Extra 8138 was delivering two loaned grain hoppers to the Co-op Atlantic Feed Plant at New Minas in this September 9, 1990, scene. The way freight was returning westbound to Kentville after interchanging at CN Rail's Rockingham yard in Halifax earlier in the day.

During the 1990s, New Minas was a regular stop for DAR way freights, which operated as required. There were two significant rail customers situated here and they represented a continuing source of revenue for the line. An average of four or five loaded grain hoppers per week were spotted at the large feed mill during the summer months. In the winter, this volume increased to eight to ten of these one-hundred-ton cars, which contained a variety of feed products, such as wheat, corn, barley, and soy-bean meal.

The main line is out of sight to the left of this photograph; caboose No. 43478, one of CP Rail's modern wide-vision types, was left on the main line while the train did its work here. On the other side of the main line, there is a spur serving the Hostess Frito-Lay plant to which, on average, there was one tank car of canola oil delivered per week. This vegetable oil was used in frying potato chips.

When radios and centralized traffic control replaced telegraphy and handwritten train orders, stations were not needed except for scheduled passenger service. When VIA passenger service was cancelled on January 15, 1990, the Wolfville station was closed. The closure spurred town planners on to meet with CP Rail to acquire the building for a new library.

The official opening of the library occurred on September 11, 1993. The event was scheduled for 2:00 PM. Ironically at 1:45 PM, the sound of a westbound train passing through Grand-Pré was heard in the distance. Steve Slipp, dressed in a borrowed conductor's uniform for a role in the ceremonies, positioned himself in plain sight on the station platform with watch in hand as Extra 1275 approached at ten miles per hour. Trainman Jim Murray, visible in the cab, and engineer Allen Russell were most interested in Steve as they leaned out the window with very puzzled expressions to study him.

Few knew that this was the last westbound train to Kentville. It dropped off two loaded grain cars in New Minas at the Co-op Atlantic Feed Plant and the loaded oil tank car at the Hostess plant and then stayed in Kentville with the caboose until Monday. It departed Kentville without fanfare. Abandonment of the rails west of New Minas became official days later, on September 23, 1993.

CPR Running rights, Bedford, 1991.

A. ROSS HARRISON

Following completion of its transcontinental line, the CPR focused on expansion to the east coast and within four years had extended their line from Montreal to Saint John, partly by building some new trackage but mostly by purchasing, leasing, or obtaining running rights agreements on existing lines. The intention was to gain access to east coast ports that offered better access to Europe, especially in the winter when Montreal was icebound.

The CPR realized very early that access to Halifax, the major eastern Canadian seaport, was vital to the railway's interests and was quite strategic in pursuing this. The process began with direct attempts to negotiate with the Intercolonial Railway and the Dominion government to gain running rights over ICR tracks from Saint John to Halifax. This failed because the diversion of revenues to the CPR was illogical.

The CPR was working on another strategy. The CPR knew about the DAR's legally binding running rights on CNR tracks into Halifax, and, c. 1890, CPR's general manager in Saint John contacted J. W. King, the W&AR's resident manager, to sign an agreement by which passengers on the W&AR's Digby–Saint John ferry would travel on their railways. This was done so when CPR's direct approach to gain access to Halifax was denied in the early 1900s, there was already a business link between the CPR and DAR; successful negotiations for the CPR's lease of the DAR followed.

Ross Harrison recorded this shot of a westbound DAR train on CN tracks at Bedford, still exercising CPR's running rights in August 1991.

Jimmy Murray was the trainman and Allen Russell was driving Extra 1274 at the Ralston Purina feed plant in Centreville on May 17, 1993. By this time, the line shown here was called the Kingsport Spur; it ended at this site.

There had been a significant number of changes that did not bode well for the DAR's survival. In 1961 the line to Kingsport beyond Steam Mill, and the Weston Branch had been abandoned. Many more changes were in the offing. In 1969 with federal funding a new ferry terminal was built at Digby and was situated well away from the DAR station.

In the 1970s, Highway 101 construction started, which accelerated the rate of decline in DAR freight and passenger traffic. The line west of Kentville was given branch line status. VIA Rail took over passenger service in 1978.

In 1986 the Mantua–Truro line was abandoned beyond the Miller's Creek Gypsum quarry. If this was not enough, a more ominous announcement was CP Rail's 1988 formation of the Canadian Atlantic Railway, an administrative unit comprising the unprofitable rail lines east of Montreal. And to make matters even worse, around that same time the trunk Highway 101 was finished from Halifax to Yarmouth, diverting even more freight and passenger traffic from the DAR.

In that same period, it was noted the DAR steel bridges were aging—with maintenance and upkeep deferred. In 1989 the federal government enacted major cuts to VIA Rail; DAR service stopped and the line west of Kentville was abandoned. In 1993 the Kentville shops were closed and servicing moved to Windsor. The sale of the DAR was one year away.

*Repairs to No. 8138;
last week of the DAR,
Hantsport, 1994.*
GARY NESS

CN required that any foreign units running on their tracks be inspected for roadworthiness before they would transfer them to Saint John. Unfortunately for CP, No. 8138 was found to have serious flange wear, making it very dangerous to haul. A normal one-inch wheel flange profile is rounded at the end. In this case, contact between the side of the railhead and the side of the flange had flattened the inner edge of the flange to a vertical line, leaving a sharp outer edge, which might easily pick a switch and cause a derailment. Close examination of the visible flange in the photo above reveals the flat surface on its inner side, which rubs on the rail head.

On August 25, 1994, the diesel was parked on the spur behind the station in Hantsport, and a heavy crane was hired to lift the front end and allow the offending four-wheel truck to be rolled out. The crane rental cost three hundred dollars per hour so time was a concern. Mike May and two men sent from Saint John were assisted by local shops crew; they blocked the rear-end wheels, lifted the nose, disconnected the truck from the locomotive, rolled it out from under the unit, lifted the truck and dropped the offending wheel-set out, rolled it away, dropped the new wheel-set onto the track, positioned it, dropped the truck onto it, then reconnected the wiring before finally rolling the new truck under the unit and connecting it. All this was accomplished in fairly short order.

Last run on the DAR, Falmouth, August 26, 1994.
GARY NESS

This was the last run on the DAR. Extra 8027 East was about to pass under the Falmouth Connector bound from Hantsport to Windsor Junction. The DAR was only one month and five days short of its one hundredth anniversary.

The train was drawn by two working units, CP RS23s Nos. 8027 and 8038, which, on August 29, would begin to work for the Windsor and Hantsport Railway (WHRC). The four diesels, Nos. 1273, 1274, 1275, and 8138, behind the RS23s, were dead-in-tow. CN would attach them to a freight train for delivery to CP Rail in Saint John. CP chose to keep those four diesels, which continued to operate for many years elsewhere in Canada.

The train departed Hantsport at 5:45 PM loaded with people. The three-man operating crew, engineer Allen Russell, conductor Carter Smith, and trainman Barry Buchanan, were in the lead unit. Carter, who was familiar with the units, drove, while Allen performed Carter's duties. Some of the new owners from Iron Road Railways (the holding company for the WHRC) rode in the cab of the second unit. They requested the RS23s be used to test drive their equipment. The RS23s set off the four CP SW1200rs diesels at Windsor Junction, picked up a grain hopper and a tank car, returned to Hantsport, set the cars off behind the station, and shut down for the weekend.

Just east of Mount Uniacke on the trip to Windsor Junction, a car had been abandoned on the tracks far from any access road. After using the radio and considering options, the lead diesel pushed the car aside, and the train continued to the Junction.

CHAPTER 7

THE WINDSOR AND HANTSPORT ERA 1994–2014

WHRC first run, Mount Denson, August 29, 1994. GARY NESS

CP RAIL AND IRON ROAD RAILWAYS LAWYERS, MANAGERS, AND OWNERS MET AT 10:00 AM ON Monday August 29, 1994, to conclude the sale of the DAR. Two train crews had been called to operate in two shifts that day. The first, early crew was sent home when talks became protracted, and the second crew took over. Carter Smith (engineer), Barry "Bucky" Buchanan (trainman), and Reg Gilby (trainman) marshalled the first train in the Hantsport yard. The first way freight to New Minas would be called for the next day.

The crew took a few minutes to roll the lead unit's front wheels over pennies, recover these souvenirs, conduct the brake test, and leave Hantsport by 6:40 PM. Iron Road president Bob Schmidt, WHRC president Dan Sabin, and WHRC manager Jim Taylor were also aboard the train for that first run as it highballed across Highway 1 at Mount Denson in the photo shown here.

The train stopped at Windsor, uncoupled the diesels from the train, uncoupled No. 8026, the lead unit, from the trailing units, Nos. 8046 and 8027, and then turned the two trailing units on the wye. The units were recoupled with No. 8027 in the lead. This manoeuvre aligned all three diesels with their long hoods pointing west, which also positioned their radiator grills for air intake at the front of the units' noses for maximum cooling during the westbound return-trip climb with a loaded train up Shaw's Bog hill to the west of Falmouth.

The official opening ceremony of the WHRC occurred on October 1, 1994—exactly one hundred years to the day after those first official trains ran on the DAR (page 19).

By 11:30 AM, a significant crowd of invited guests and members of the public had gathered. Bob Schmidt (second from left), president of Iron Roads, made opening remarks then introduced the special guests and dignitaries. WHRC employees, wearing new maroon WHRC caps, were on the running board of No. 8046, which had a new maroon paint job.

Fred Green, former general manager of the CAR and then senior vice-president with CP Rail (and later its president and CEO), signed a Document of Record, which was then read by Robbie Harrison, the Kings South Member of the Legislative Assembly. The special guests boarded the locomotive, which then moved forward, cutting the ribbon. Those across the front of the diesel include, from the left, George Cooper, Bob Schmidt, Robbie Harrison, Dan Sabin, Pete Collins, and John Murphy (Member of Parliament, Annapolis Valley–Hants). Visible on the side footboard are WHRC employees Brian Aulenbach, Les Garvey, Danny Trider, Steve Spicer, Mike Saunders, Graham Selby, Peter Laing, Barry Buchanan, and Jim Murray. Not visible behind them are Carter Smith, Neil Marquis, Peter Johnstone, and Jim Taylor.

After the ceremony, the assembled guests, including the public, were invited to ride a special excursion train which had a borrowed VIA Rail stainless steel coach; it required four trips to accommodate everyone.

Two if By Sea *movie scenes shot on WHRC, Windsor, 1995.* GARY NESS

Scenes for a Hollywood movie were shot in mid-June 1995 in Wolfville, Hantsport, and Windsor. Local residents were invited to audition for bystander roles, and to add to the excitement, the movie Two if By Sea brought Hollywood actor Sandra Bullock to the Valley. A scene was needed inside an Amtrak coach as a train ran beside a supposed stretch of Maine seacoast. The Windsor causeway was the perfect site and rented VIA equipment was in Windsor on Saturday June 24, 1995. Filming of railway scenes began on Sunday at the Hantsport station, where the name board read "Narragansett." The train was parked in front of the station while camera and lighting gear was set up in and on their "hero car."

The consist for the train included lightly disguised "Amtrak" 5656 (VIA Chateau Maisonneuve No. 8217); Hero Car No. 8144

(ex-Amtrak coach, now VIA); "Amtrak" No. 8147 (ex-Amtrak coach, now VIA); WHRC eighty-five-foot flatcar loaded with a generator and other equipment; and the WHRC caboose. VIA sleeping cars, No. 3145 (Chateau Dollier) and No. 7872 (Chateau LaSalle) were on a siding beside the station. The train left Hantsport at 10:40 AM, and crept along to avoid damage from trackside brush to the platform and wiring on the outside of the hero car. Run-by filming at Akins Crossing preceded the filming on the causeway, which involved numerous run-bys from the Falmouth Connector to the Windsor station, all with a line of police cars chasing alongside the hero car on the causeway (visible behind the diesel). Filming ended in Wolfville the next day.

WHRC grain movements, Greenwich, 1995.

GARY NESS

Grain movements continued as a significant part of freight traffic in the early days of the WHRC. This train, shown at Greenwich, was on a renovated siding that had almost sunk out of sight by the last days of the DAR. Upon buying the line, the WHRC raised the siding—track and ties—out of the mud and shored up the siding to receive hundred-ton loads at the Shur-Gain silos, visible here, on August 9, 1995. (I noted "what a difference a year makes" on the back of this picture because the scene was so busy.) This way freight was returning to Windsor with nine empties from the Co-Op Atlantic Feed Plant in New Minas and would pick up another seven cars here in Greenwich.

Unfortunately, this freight business was ephemeral with grain movements shifting back and forth between trucking companies and the railway. It seemed that with each year the railway lost more ground in this struggle. However, the final blow was delivered not by trucks, but by time. The aging Gaspereaux River bridge was due for inspection soon and the W&AR knew the significant repairs were too expensive. Without the inspection and upgrades, the line would be unable to access the rails west of that bridge. The decision was made to build a grain-unloading auger in Windsor and to truck grain from that hub. In that way, the railway was at least able to continue a grain-freight operation on the line from Windsor Junction to Windsor.

A typical day? Falmouth, 1997.
GARY NESS

The first gypsum run of the day on April 24, 1997, was about to pass under the Falmouth Connector and was in notch 8, the highest throttle setting, as it accelerated towards Shaw's Bog hill. The ALCOs were belching their usual smoke—a trait that made rail fans smile and environmentalists cringe.

Clearly this was not a typical train. The gypsum crew's day began in unusual fashion, taking this loaded gypsum train and an inserted special train to Hantsport. The train included four WHRC diesels, Nos. 8038, 8041, 8027, and 8023, plus a former VIA coach still in VIA's blue and yellow scheme, the WHRC caboose No. 150, and the loaded gypsum hoppers. The train proceeded to Hantsport where the gypsum loads were set off on a siding in the yard. Three units then continued the normal gypsum run.

The special train was marshalled after further switching movements, with No. 8038 in the lead, after which the train was spotted in front of the station where invited guests boarded, and then it departed to Grand-Pré where a meeting regarding tourist excursions was convened.

After dropping the passengers, the train crew ran west to Wolfville for a coffee stop at Tim Hortons, then west to a passing siding where the diesel and caboose were switched around for the eastbound trip back. The train then returned to Grand-Pré and delivered the special guests and dignitaries back to Windsor later that afternoon.

WHRC excursion trains, Falmouth, 1997.
GARY NESS

The DAR and its predecessors had a long history of excursion train operation dating back to the earliest times (pages 11, 39, 44, and 137). Fittingly, the WHRC continued that tradition. After the success of their first excursion trains on the opening day in 1994, WHRC excursion trains were fairly commonplace, accommodating special guests, dignitaries, business associates, and the public. The public response led to the purchase of unique equipment, including two open-air observation cars that came from the Great Smoky Mountains Railroad where the original names were Nantahala and Hiwassee. Renamed EVANGELINE and GABRIEL, they were repainted in maroon, gold, and grey livery, in keeping with the line's traditions.

The WHRC's Evangeline Express ran during the summer of 1997 as a pilot project. In addition to the open-air cars, the usual consist included locomotives on either end, a former VIA coach, and their former CP wide-vision caboose, painted maroon. On Friday, July 4, a special test train ran from Windsor to Wolfville carrying invited guests, families, dignitaries, working employees, and musicians. Over the next two days, six revenue trips of the Acadia Days Special ran from Windsor to Wolfville, then shuttled three times between Hantsport and Wolfville, before tying up in Windsor.

The trains continued to operate on weekends throughout the summer period. The pilot project produced mixed results. The revenue generated was positive, but the schedule placed a burden on staff: members worked regular weekday hours and weekends as well. No solution could be found and the train did not operate regularly after that.

WHRC caboose No. 150, Windsor, 1995.
GARY NESS

WHRC caboose No. 150 was originally CP Rail No. 434678, a yellow, steel, wide-vision caboose built in 1981 by CP Rail at Angus Shops as part of the 434675–434734 series of cabooses. It was one of two modern, steel, wide-vision CP Rail cabooses, including No. 434676, that was sent to the DAR in 1990 for use on gypsum trains and was part of the equipment sold to the WHRC in 1994.

Soon after the WHRC purchased the DAR, the caboose was renumbered and repainted in traditional Land of Evangeline and DAR fashion, and in WHRC's own version of the maroon, grey, and gold CP/DAR schemes. RS23 No. 8046 was treated similarly; it was their first paint job and was done under the Highway 101 overpass

at Falmouth since the shops were not yet available and timing was of the essence to have the locomotive ready for the official opening in October.

The caboose also received the name Christine Schmidt in honour of the daughter of the new owner, Bob Schmidt. The name is visible just below the cupola window.

These new WHRC paint schemes were well received. The traditional colours, the naming, and the show of pride of ownership followed a number of fondly remembered, long-time DAR traditions.

The caboose was used by the WHRC for display at the Windsor headquarters and on numerous excursions and other special trains.

WHRC Roster.
GARY NESS

ON JUNE 4, 2006, former CN GP9 No. 1430 was leading WHRC RS23 No. 8042 on a freight train just east of Windsor, bound for Windsor Junction.

The WHRC owned an eclectic collection of locomotives. Eight RS23 road switchers were part of the agreement to buy the DAR; these were former CP Rail Nos. 8026, 8027, 8036, 8037, 8038, 8041, 8042, and 8046.

In 1995 the WHRC purchased former passenger diesels, VIA FPA4 No. 6786 and FPB4 No. 6867, for their ALCO parts. They were delivered in November. WHRC also purchased VIA FPA4 Nos. 6761, 6763, 6765, and 6783, plus FPB4 Nos. 6861 and 6862; they were never delivered but traded to CP Rail for five more RS23s, Nos. 8019, 8023, 8034, 8040, and 8045. Some of the thirteen RS23s were used to work the line, while others were used as needed for parts.

Starting in 2005 with the RS23s failing, two CN GMD1s, Nos. 1423 and 1430, were leased for short periods in 2005 and 2006 respectively, and then returned to CN. In 2006 twelve RS23s were scrapped; No. 8036 followed in 2007.

In 2006 four GP9RM rebuilt diesels were leased from Central Manitoba Railway (CEMR): Nos. 4011, (ex-CN 4011, ex-CN 4594); 4012, (ex-CN 4008, ex-CN 4597); 4013, (ex-CN 4013, ex-CN 4494); and 4014, (ex-CN 4001, ex-CN 4567).

With the expiration of the CEMR lease in 2011, the WHRC purchased two GE (General Electric) B23-7 diesels, No. 1968 (ex-Nashville & Eastern 1968 from NREX [National Railway Equipment Company], ex-Conrail 1968) and No. 4079 (ex-Nashville & Eastern 4079 from NREX, ex-Norfolk Southern 4079, ex-Conrail 1999).

The future of the WHRC may take a beneficial turn. The creation of the WHRC was part of a North America-wide trend. All major railways were divesting themselves of deteriorating, money-losing branch lines, preferably by selling them to short lines that would continue to supply the large railways with traffic because the short lines could operate with lower overhead costs. For example, short lines were able to pay lower wages and assign employees a variety of jobs based on the railway's needs. Collective agreements with the major railways made such changes impossible, but the short line advantages provided considerable savings that then allowed the smaller companies to eke out a profit.

The early WHRC continued doing much of what the late-stage DAR did, including handling gypsum trains, grain movements to feed mills, pulpwood shipments, and the occasional tank cars of cooking oil to the Hostess plant in New Minas. The mainstay of their operation continued to be gypsum, which was not readily shipped by truck to Hantsport. However, all other freight was under pressure from trucking and there was a continuing shift in traffic on the Halifax–Windsor route as the contracts to move these commodities shifted back and forth between trucks and trains.

The apparent demise of the WHRC came suddenly in 2011 when the Fundy Gypsum Company closed its mines due to the depressed housing market in the United States. The WHRC has been mothballed since then. However, the long-standing lease of the Windsor Branch expired in 2013, and CN, which still owns the Branch, gave public notice of intent to abandon or sell the Windsor Branch to a buyer who would "benefit" CN Rail. Talks between CN and WHRC owner Bob Schmidt were ongoing when this was written in early 2014. Hopefully, we will continue to see trains in the Valley.

APPENDIX A: A GUIDE TO RAILWAY ACRONYMS, PARLANCE, AND TERMS

RAILWAY NAMES AND ACRONYMS

CAR: Canadian Atlantic Railway, name of eastern portions of CP Rail after 1988.

CNR: Canadian National Railway.

CPR: Canadian Pacific Railway.

CP RAIL: name of the CPR 1968–1996.

CVR: Cornwallis Valley Railway, a line from Kentville to Kingsport, part of the DAR.

DAR: Dominion Atlantic Railway.

ICR: Intercolonial Railway, built and operated by the Government of Canada, an outcome of Confederation and a need to link the founding provinces by rail, later became part of the CNR.

MR: Midland Railway, a line from Windsor to Truro, became part of the DAR.

NSR: Nova Scotia Railway, built and operated initially by the Nova Scotia government, later became part of the ICR, then the CNR.

W&AR: Windsor and Annapolis Railway, a line from Windsor to, became part of the DAR.

WCR: Western Counties Railway, a line from Annapolis Royal to Yarmouth, became part of the DAR.

WESTON BRANCH: A line from Centreville to Weston, also known as the North Mountain Branch, part of the DAR.

WINDSOR BRANCH (OF THE NSR): a line from Windsor to Windsor Junction where it connected to the CNR (formerly the ICR, formerly the NSR), became part of the DAR.

WHRC: Windsor and Hantsport Railway (Company), the new name of the DAR after its sale, the line ran from New Minas to Halifax with a spur to the Fundy Gypsum quarries at Mantua (pronounced "man-too-ay" or "man-oo-ay" locally), east of Windsor.

Y&AR: Yarmouth and Annapolis Railway, a short-lived name for the WCR just prior to the formation of the DAR.

STEAM LOCOMOTIVE NOMENCLATURE / WHEEL ARRANGEMENTS AND COMMON NAMES

The Whyte notation for describing steam locomotives was based on wheel arrangement. The system referred to the *lead* or *pilot wheels* at the front of the locomotive, the large *drive wheels* (or *drivers*) that propelled the locomotive, and the *trailing wheels* at the rear of the engine beneath the locomotive cab.

An 0-6-0 or *switcher/switch engine* type (page 71) had no leading wheels (hence the number zero but pronounced like the letter, "o"), six drive wheels (three on each side, hence six), and no trailing truck at the back (another zero), hence the 0-6-0 label; this wheel type was used mostly for yard duties as *switchers*.

The 4-4-0 or American type (page 9) had four leading wheels, four drive wheels, and no trailing wheels.

The 2-6-0 or Mogul type (page 26) had two leading wheels, six drive wheels, and no trailing wheels.

The 4-6-0 or Ten-wheeler type (page 30) had four leading wheels, six drive wheels, and no trailing wheels.

A 4-6-2 or Pacific type (page 84) had four leading wheels, six drive wheels, and two trailing wheels.

CPR LOCOMOTIVE CLASSIFICATIONS

Over time the CPR built or purchased many locomotives of various wheel arrangements. For example, the CPR owned over one thousand Ten-wheelers.

The D2, D4, and D6 classes of Ten-wheelers were CPR designations for three different types of small 4-6-0s; No. 470 was a D4. The D6 class was another CPR class of small 4-6-0s with numbers in the 500s. Additionally, the acquisition of any class of locomotives often involved different builders or a series of purchases over time. For example, there were four classes of the D6: the D6a, D6b, D6c, and D6d groups, which were built by various companies over several years.

D10: A CPR class for a type of 4-6-0 or Ten-wheeler that was larger and heavier, with numbers in the 900s, 1000s, and 1100s on the DAR.

G1: A CPR class for one type of 4-6-2 or Pacific with numbers in the 2200s.

G2: A CPR designation for another type of 4-6-2 with numbers in the 2500s and 2600s

DIESEL NOMENCLATURE

ALCO S3: The third of a series of different diesel switchers built by the American Locomotive Company (hence ALCO). The S3 models were small, light diesels of 1000hp and not suited to the heavy DAR gypsum trains.

GMW SW1200rs: Built by General Motors Works, a diesel switcher design with 1200hp but modified for road switcher use. A typical switcher was not geared or built for high-speed running. The "rs" modifications allowed for yard switching and main line running.

DAYLINER / RDC: Built by Budd Locomotive Company, the Rail Diesel Cars (RDCs) came in several numbered configurations. The RDC1 featured an interior filled with seating for passengers. Other configurations (RDC2, RDC3, etc.) divided the interior into compartments for carrying luggage and different uses. The term *Dayliner* was the popular name for the RDCs.

RAILWAY TERMS AND PRACTICES

MILES AND TONS

North American railways rely on the English/Imperial (United States) system for units of distance and weight; therefore, Canadian railways never switched to metric. There are still distance markers—called mile boards or mile posts—along most railways. These indicate the distances along a given stretch of track. The employee timetables still cite all distances in miles. Similarly, weights are cited in pounds and tons.

DIVISIONS AND SUBDIVISIONS

Railways are divided into these operating subunits, which appear in the employee timetable. Typically a subdivision, or sub, is the portion of the railway over which a train crew operates before being replaced by a new crew. A division is a collection of subs.

WYE

A three-sided triangular track formation with switches at each corner is a wye. It could be a junction or used for reversing direction. Turning a locomotive involved pulling ahead into a corner then reversing out of each corner on the other track until the locomotive came to rest at its starting point; it would then be facing in the opposite direction.

UNIFORM CODE OF OPERATING RULES

A collection of general rules governing railway operations is available as a small pocket-sized booklet.

EMPLOYEE TIMETABLES

A highly detailed set of instructions guide the operation of all types of trains, including scheduled passenger runs, scheduled and unscheduled freight trains, and mixed trains. These timetables indicated operating speeds, availability of water and coal, allowable weights of locomotives on sections of track, and a host of other important instructions about communications, and so on. These were usually updated twice yearly. The public received copies of only the public timetable, the schedule for passenger trains.

TRAIN ORDERS

These were issued to the operating crews of every train. Before radios, train orders were paper copies that crews read aloud to one another.

SUPERIOR AND INFERIOR TRAINS

By convention, even-numbered trains in the employee timetable were eastward and superior while westbound trains were odd-numbered and inferior. The terms *superior* and *inferior* indicate that westbound trains, those moving in the Halifax-to-Yarmouth direction, had to take the siding for meets with scheduled eastbound trains; trains were assigned superiority by train order, superior class (conferred by the operating timetable), or by superior direction.

Extra trains were not included in the timetable but were run as needed. They were identified as an extra by white flags mounted on either side at the front of the locomotive. A green flag was used to identify a second section of a scheduled train. *Scheduled Extras* were trains that were not expected to run every day, but they had been allocated a time in the operating schedule for seasonal and other such trains. *Work Extras* were trains operating on company business, such as doing repairs or inspecting the line.

Jigging, drop-by, or *flying switch moves* were railway terms used to describe train movements when crews were confronted with switching at a facing point switch. Trains were assembled with cars behind the locomotive and obviously it was easier to set cars off in sidings with the switch pointed at the rear of the train, a trailing point switch.

When the locomotive had to set cars off at a location where there was a facing point switch, and no passing siding to run around the back end of the train to push a car into the siding, jigging was used. This involved stopping the train, uncoupling any cars behind the car to be set off, then starting the locomotive and attached cars toward the switch, which remained aligned to let the locomotive pass by on the main line. The car destined to be in the siding was cut off on-the-fly and continued to roll slowly forward while the locomotive accelerated quickly past the switch. Once the locomotive cleared the switch, it was "thrown" (realigned) for the siding, and the car rolled into the siding and was braked to a stop at the correct point. Timing was obviously critical.

Running light or a *caboose hop* was railway jargon for a locomotive running alone or with only a caboose attached; the term *light* referred to the weight pulled by locomotive.

In the hole was railway jargon for being in a passing siding to allow another train to pass.

Notch 8 was the highest throttle setting; the locomotive throttle had eight notches. An engineer was said to "notch" the speed and power up and down.

APPENDIX B

INTRODUCTION TO STEAM ROSTERS

DEFINITIVE "ALL-TIME" ROSTERS OF THE DAR AND ITS PREDECESSOR lines may never be finalized. Omer Lavallée, the highly respected CPR archivist and historian, wrote a most comprehensive overview of the reasons for this in his book *Canadian Pacific Steam Locomotives*. He noted that from the time CPR leased the line in 1912 to August 2004, company-owned motive power was supervised by the CPR's Mechanical Department in Montreal. In 1912 at the takeover, the DAR had thirty locomotives: twenty-seven of these were a hodgepodge of former DAR types and three were ex-CPR, bought from the CPR by the DAR in 1910 and 1911. The CPR began to retire the twenty-seven DAR types in 1917, and replaced them with CPR types that were sold to the line, renumbered and named in typical DAR fashion. All of this was documented in CPR records. However, names were not recorded by the CPR and often passed to other locomotives as engines were scrapped. After 1937 CPR policies changed; locomotives sold to the DAR retained CPR numbers, but the "Land of Evangeline" herald on the tender side-panel was still allowed. Naming of locomotives—never officially sanctioned—ended with the outbreak of World War Two in 1939.

By far the greatest challenge is related to tracing locomotives that were on the DAR for short periods to cope with temporary traffic increases because they were loaned or leased, and these transfers were not recorded in CPR files. CPR policy stated that these locomotives were not to be identified as DAR locomotives, but when they stayed long enough to require shopping, repainting as DAR units sometimes occurred anyway, as a matter of pride. Thus, the most reliable record of their DAR sojourn as loaned equipment is in the photographic records.

Naming of locomotives was not well documented either; CPR records after the takeover referred only to the locomotive numbers, although the use of names was still allowed, unofficially. Hence, name assignments and re-assignments by date and locomotive(s) were not complete. Also, names and numbers were changed and swapped, further complicating an accurate roster.

The DAR steam roster could easily be described as a series of overlapping stages characterized by the presence on the line of specific groups of locomotives. These occurred in several eras, commencing with the early 4-4-0s (and two 2-6-0s) built or acquired before 1894 for the predecessor lines; the small 4-4-0s and 4-6-0s built or bought by the DAR between 1894 and 1912 (some of which lasted until the early 1940s); the era of the small CPR D6 4-6-0s sold, loaned, or leased to the DAR after the 1912 CPR takeover to the early 1940s; and the "modern era" of the "larger" CPR power—the D10 4-6-0s and G2 4-6-2s starting in 1937 and ending in 1961.

The histories of the predecessor lines have been included because those early railways were so inextricably intertwined with the early DAR that ignoring them was impossible. For example, steam locomotive numbers from 1894 to 1912 were two digits and the locomotives bore names, a continuation of the numbering and naming patterns of the lines that were amalgamated to form the DAR. The rosters of those same lines, the Windsor Branch of the Windsor and Annapolis Railway, the Western Counties Railway, the Cornwallis Valley Railway, and the Midland Railway, all of which contributed locomotives to the early DAR roster, are included.

I have not attempted to present a technical, detail-laden accounting of each locomotive.

ROSTERS OF THE PREDECESSOR LINES (PRIOR TO 1894)

I have several lists of early locomotives on the various constituent lines and while there are lots of similarities, there is incomplete agreement among them.

Marguerite Woodworth's book *History of the Dominion Atlantic Railway* is full of details about the DAR predecessor lines, and may be the best source on this complex topic. Careful reading of other documents may also help in getting roster information, but there were unexplained inconsistencies among them.

The following underscores why reservations about "definitive rosters" persist.

THE ROSTER OF THE WINDSOR BRANCH, NOVA SCOTIA RAILWAY

A January 20, 1856, report indicated that three locos were assigned to the Windsor Branch. Details about No. 1 were not found, but Nos. 2 GASPARD LEMARCHANT and 3 JOSEPH HOWE arrived in 1855 and were sold to the W&AR in 1869. Both were 4-2-0 bicycle types, built by Neilson in 1855. Apparently both of them were rebuilt from 4-2-0T to 2-2-0T types (that is, they had a single pair of drive wheels).

ROSTER OF THE WINDSOR AND ANNAPOLIS RAILWAY, PART 1: THE BROAD GAUGE LOCOMOTIVES

There were two rosters for the W&AR, which was broad gauge until 1875; after that the broad gauge engines were traded for a like number of standard gauge units.

SIR GASPARD LEMARCHANT (ex-NSR 2) may have been renamed MALICEET on the W&AR; JOSEPH HOWE (ex-NSR 3) may have been named MIC-MAC on the W&AR; ST LAWRENCE was a 4-4-0, (ex-Grand Trunk 4); EVANGELINE, GABRIEL, and GASPEREAUX (1868); and MINNEHAHA, HIAWATHA, and GRAND PRE (1869) were 4-4-0s built by Fox Walker in the years indicated; LIGHTNING (ex-Great Western (UK) No. 2) was a 4-4-0 built in 1853; and ST CROIX was a 4-4-0.

Various inventories of the time list these in different orders and their numbers are subject to dispute. For example, one 1873 inventory moved GRAND PRE to third spot and MINNEHAHA into sixth. Another replaces MINNEHAHA with BLOMIDON and adds BASIL, BENEDICT, MINNEHAHA to the swap list.

ROSTER OF THE WINDSOR AND ANNAPOLIS RAILWAY, PART 2: THE STANDARD GAUGE LOCOMOTIVES

The above listed broad gauge locos were traded for ICR standard gauge engines as part of a deal with the federal government. All were 4-4-0 types.

> 1 EVANGELINE: ex-ICR 21, ex-NSR 21, later DAR 14, sold to New Brunswick Railway
> 2 GABRIEL: ex-ICR 22, ex-NSR 22, later DAR 13
> 3 HIAWATHA: ex-ICR 23, ex-NSR 23, later DAR 3
> 4 BLOMIDON: ex-ICR 32, ex-E&AR (*) 9 (OSSEKEAG), later DAR 4
> 5 GRAND PRE: ex-ICR 32, ex-E&AR (APOHAQUI), later DAR 5
> 6 GASPEREAUX: ex-ICR 24, ex-NSR 24, later DAR 6
> 7 BASIL 4-4-0 built in 1875
> 8 BENEDICT
> 9 MINNEHAHA: later DAR 9

(*) E&NA was the European and North American Railway in New Brunswick

ROSTER OF THE WINDSOR AND ANNAPOLIS RAILWAY, PART 3: ACQUISITIONS AFTER THE TRADE:

All the following were 4-4-0s.

> 10 KENTVILLE: later DAR 12 (page 9)
> 11 ST EULALIE: later DAR 9
> 12 ACADIA: later DAR 11
> 13 QUEEN MAB: ex-CVR, later DAR 1
> 14 ATALANTA: later DAR 16
> 15 OBERON: later DAR 19
> 16 TITANIA: later DAR 20
> 17 FORTUNA: later DAR 21
> 18 REGINA: later DAR 23
> 19 CERISE: later DAR 22

ROSTER OF THE WESTERN COUNTIES RAILWAY, PART 1: OPERATING THE WINDSOR BRANCH (THE "EASTERN" DIVISION OF THE WCR)

Relations between the WCR and the W&AR were tumultuous at best during the time the WCR operated the Windsor Branch. As a result the WCR could not transfer rolling stock from one part of its operations to the other on W&AR tracks. In essence, the Western Counties Railway operated two completely separate rosters at that time.

There were two 2-6-0 or Mogul types; WINDSOR and FRANK KILLAM were reported as a 4-4-0s in some cases but were both Mogul types according to sources. The other two eastern WCR locomotives, HALIFAX and YARMOUTH, were 4-4-0s. All four of these marooned in 1879 in Halifax at the ICR roundhouse near the Richmond station, when the W&AR resumed control. They were sold to New Brunswick and Canada Railway.

ROSTER OF THE WESTERN COUNTIES RAILWAY, PART 2: THE ORIGINAL OR "WESTERN" LINE

All the following were 4-4-0s.
> 1 PIONEER: later DAR 2
> 2 CORNWALLIS: later DAR 7 (page 11)
> 3 WESTERN: later DAR 10 (page 17)
> 4 ANNAPOLIS: later DAR 15
> 5 YARMOUTH: ex-WCR x, later DAR 17
> 6 DIGBY: later DAR 18
> 7 ? (No data found)
> 8 WEYMOUTH: later DAR 8 (page 13)

ROSTER OF THE MIDLAND RAILWAY

> 1 TRURO: 4-4-0, later DAR 31

> 2 WINDSOR: 4-4-0, later DAR 30

> 3 BROOKLYN: 4-4-0, later DAR 29 (page 21)

> 4 PIONEER 2-6-0, later DAR 28

ROSTER DAR 1894–1912: FORMATION TO LEASE BY CPR

> 1 QUEEN MAB: 4-4-0, ex-W&AR 13

> 2 PIONEER: 4-4-0, ex-WCR 1

> 3 HIAWATHA: 4-4-0, ex-NSR 23, then ICR 23, then W&AR 3

> 4 BLOMIDON: 4-4-0, ex-E&NAR (*) 9, named OSSEKEAG, then W&AR 4

> 5 GRAND PRE: 4-4-0, ex-E&NAR 13, then W&AR 5

> 6 GASPEREAUX: 4-4-0, ex-NSR, then ICR, then W&AR 6

> 7 GEORGE B. DOANE: (CORNWALLIS?) 4-4-0, ex-WCR, then Y&AR 2

> 8 WEYMOUTH: 4-4-0, ex-WCR, then Y&AR 8

> 9 MINNEHAHA (ST EULALIE): 4-4-0, ex-W&AR 9

> 10 WESTERN (KENTVILLE): 4-4-0, ex-WCR, then Y&AR 3

> 11 ACADIA: 4-4-0, ex-W&AR 12

> 12 KENTVILLE: 4-4-0, ex-W&AR 10

> 13 GABRIEL: 4-4-0, ex-NSR 22, then W&AR 2

> 14 EVANGELINE: 4-4-0, ex-NSR 21, then W&AR 1

> 15 ANNAPOLIS: 4-4-0, ex-WCR, then Y&AR 4

> 16 ATALANTA: 4-4-0, ex-W&AR 14

> 17 YARMOUTH: 4-4-0, ex-WCR, then Y&AR 5

> 18 DIGBY: 4-4-0, ex-WCR, then Y&AR 6

> 19 OBERON: 4-4-0, ex-W&AR 15

> 20 TITANIA: 4-4-0, ex-W&AR 16

> 21 FORTUNA: 4-4-0, ex-W&AR 17

> 22 CERESE: 4-4-0, ex-WCR 7, named W. R. Moody, then W&AR 19

> 23 REGINA: 4-4-0, ex-W&AR 18

> 24 LADY LATOUR: 4-4-0 built for DAR

> 25 PONTGRAVE, then STRATHCONA: 4-4-0 built for DAR

> 26 PRESIDENT, then GOVENOR COX, then KENT: 4-4-0 built for DAR

> 27 CANADA: 4-4-0 built for DAR

> 28 PIONEER: 2-6-0, ex-ICR (No.?), then MR 4

> 29 BROOKLYN: 4-4-0, ex-GTR No. 300, then 420, then MR 3

> 29 (2nd) ANNAPOLIS: 4-6-0, ex-CPR type D2b No. 7276 (on loan briefly according to Lavallée)

> 30 WINDSOR: 4-4-0, ex-GTR 192, then 261, then MR 2

> 31 TRURO: 4-4-0, ex-GTR No. 301, then 421, then MR 1

> 32 BLOMIDON: 4-6-0 built for DAR(*)

> 33 GLOOSCAP: 4-6-0 built for DAR(*)

> 34 GASPEREAUX: 4-6-0, ex-CPR 310

> 35 GABRIEL: 4-6-0, ex-CPR 319

> 36 BASIL: 4-6-0, ex-CPR 320

(*) Nos. 32 and 33 were the DAR's last order of new motive power.

THE DAR STEAM ROSTER: THE CPR YEARS 1912–1940, PART 1

At the time of the sale to the CPR, the roster included thirty DAR locomotives as follows:

4-4-0 AMERICAN TYPES

> 7 CORNWALLIS

> 8 WEYMOUTH (page 13)

> 9 ST EULALIE

> 10 WESTERN

2-6-0 Mogul type

4-6-0 Ten-wheeler types

The years immediately after the CPR acquired the DAR were dedicated to upgrading the line to CPR standards. This included sale or retirement of some of the DAR stable of small locomotives and replacement with CPR 4-6-0 types. In 1937 CPR began a full-scale replacement of these smaller locomotives. By 1939–1940 most of these were retired, sold, or scrapped.

As with other parts of the DAR roster, this list is based on incomplete records that note locomotives sold by the CPR. Photographic evidence provides the only other verifiable sources. Thus, compiling a roster is a challenging task that may never be entirely accurate.

THE DAR STEAM ROSTER: THE CPR YEARS 1912–1940, PART 2

The following are CPR 4-6-0s that were sold to the DAR.

D2 4-6-0 type

D6 4-6-0 type

- 44 (second): ex-Quebec Central 44; replaced 44 (first) (pages 53, 54, 65, 72)
- 45 CLEMENTSPORT: later renamed ALEXANDER, later renumbered DAR 503 ALEXANDER, ex-CPR 503
- 45 (second): ex-Quebec Central 45, found unacceptable and returned

D4 4-6-0 TYPE
- 385
- 387
- 470

D6 4-6-0 TYPE
- 500 MEMBERTOU (page 39)
- 502 POUTRINCOURT (page 47)
- 503 CLEMENTSPORT (page 46)
- 504 HALIFAX (page 69)
- 521 HALIFAX
- 530 LESCARBOT
- 531 BENEDICT, later NASCARENE
- 534 PONTGRAVE
- 537 EVANGELINE, later FRONSAC
- 538 GRANDFONTAINE
- 540 MASCARENE
- 544 HEBERT (pages 50, 51)
- 547 CHAMPLAIN
- 552 DIEREVILLE, later MEMBERTOU

- 555 NICHOLSON (page 77)
- 556 CHAMPDORE, later MOUNT DENSON (pages 32, 40, 41, 44)

THE DAR STEAM ROSTER: THE CPR YEARS 1912–1940, PART 3

The following are CPR small 4-6-0s that were loaned or leased to the DAR. In each instance, the presence on the DAR of the locomotives listed below has been verified by photographs.

D4 4-6-0 TYPE
- 365
- 379
- 380
- 382
- 384
- 385
- 387
- 470 (pages 62, 73)

D6 4-6-0 TYPE
- 501 DEVONSHIRE
- 518 POUTRINCOURT
- 519 (page 70)
- 520 CHAMPLAIN

- 528
- 532 D'AULNAY
- 545 HOWE
- 550
- 557 SUBERCASE

D10 4-6-0 TYPE

The following are CPR large 4-6-0s that were sold, loaned or leased to the DAR.

Sold to the DAR
- 903
- 999 (pages 50, 51, 55, 76, 85)
- 1018 DEMONTS
- 1020 (page 107)
- 1027 (front cover)
- 1040
- 1041 MEMBERTOU
- 1046 (pages 8, 114, 115, 116)
- 1067
- 1077
- 1079
- 1089
- 1090 DERAZILLY
- 1092 (pages 85, 86)
- 1111

Loaned or leased to the DAR
- 929
- 1015

> 1038 (pages 82, 111)

> 1050 (page 91)

> 1101 (page 56)

The following are CPR 4-6-2s that were sold, loaned, or leased to the DAR.

G1 4-6-2 TYPE SOLD TO THE DAR

> 2209 (pages 112, 113, 121)

G2 4-6-2 TYPE SOLD TO THE DAR

> 2501 (page 118)

> 2511 SUBERCASE (page 64)

> 2516 (page 106)

> 2526

> 2551 (pages 58, 84, 89, 105)

> 2552 HALIBURTON (pages 50, 51, 57, 88)

> 2629 (page 119)

G2 4-6-2 TYPE LOANED OR LEASED TO THE DAR

> 2500 (page vii)

> 2505

> 2515

> 2526

> 2528 (pages 83, 93)

> 2617 (pages 90, 94, 95, 97, 98)

> 2627 (pages x, 87)

> 2665 (pages 96, 97, 99)

The following are CPR 0-6-0 that were sold, loaned, or leased to the DAR.

U2 0-6-0 TYPE LOANED OR LEASED TO THE DAR

> 6058

U3 TYPE SOLD TO THE DAR

> 6189

> 6227 (page 71)

U3 TYPE LOANED OR LEASED TO THE DAR

> 6109 (page 35)

> 6161

ORIGINS OF THE NAMES USED BY THE DAR AND ITS PREDECESSOR RAILWAYS

The DAR and its predecessor lines were famous for their individuality. A famous example of this was their long-lasting practice of naming their locomotives; it drew a lot of attention. All UPPER CASE letters are used in presenting locomotive names in a number of reliable sources, and the format is used here as well.

ACADIA: English equivalent of the original French name, *Acadie*.

ALEXANDER: William Alexander rebuilt Port Royal after the British captured it from the French.

ANNAPOLIS: Western terminus of the W&AR; eastern terminus of the WCR.

ATALANTA: From Greek mythology, the Huntress.

AVON: Nova Scotia river, mouth is at Windsor.

BASIL: Blacksmith in Longfellow's epic poem *Evangeline*.

BEAR RIVER: Nova Scotia river; anglicized name thought to originate from *Riviere d'Hebert*

BENEDICT: Evangeline's father in Longfellow's *Evangeline*.

BLOMIDON: English elision of "Blow-me-down," early maps' label for the eastern cape of the North Mountain. Attributed to hydrographer Desbarres.

BOSCAWEN: Admiral, privateer, captured a French fleet of thirty-seven ships.

BROOKLYN: Nova Scotia town on the Midland Railway.

BYNG: Viscount Byng, Governor General of Canada 1921–1926.

CADILLAC: Dwelt in Nova Scotia prior to moving inland; founded the city of Detroit.

CAPT ARGALL: Destroyed Port Royal on behalf of its rival, Jamestown, Virginia.

CANADA: The significance is obvious.

CERISE: French for "cherry" and refers to a colour, "deep pinkish red," which may be a reference to the magenta colour used by the W&AR.

CHAMPDORE: Sieur De Champdore, a founder of *Acadie* in 1604.

CHAMPLAIN: Leading founder of Port Royal at the mouth of the Annapolis River, the first permanent European settlement north of the Gulf of Mexico.

CLEMENTSPORT: Nova Scotia town.

CORNWALLIS: Governor of Nova Scotia in the mid-1700s; established Halifax as his headquarters in 1749.

D'AULNAY: Sieur d'Aulnay, governor of *Acadie*, 1635–1650.

DERAZILLY: Isaac de Razilly, governor of *Acadie* 1632–1635 and founder of LaHave.

DEMONTS: Timothe Pierre du Guast deMonts, accompanied Champlain to Port Royal; first governor of Acadia.

DENYS: Commerce builder for *Acadie* fishery, lumber, and fur trades.

DEVONSHIRE: Duke of Devonshire, Governor General of Canada, 1916–1921.

DIEREVILLE: Early pioneer and historian in the late 1600s.

DIGBY: British admiral; brought 1,500 Empire Loyalists to found the Nova Scotia town of Digby in 1785.

EVANGELINE: Heroine of Longfellow's *Evangeline.*

FORTUNA: From Roman mythology, Goddess of Chance.

FRONSAC: Nicholas Denys, Sieur de Fronsac, developed early trade in fish, lumber, and furs in *Acadie.*

GABRIEL: Heroine's beau in Longfellow's *Evangeline.*

GASPEREAUX: A river where Acadians were loaded onto British ships during the expulsion.

GLOOSCAP: Primary god (Kuloskap) of the Mi'kmaq when the French arrived in 1604; he resided at Blomidon.

GOVERNOR COX: sometime (erroneously) reported as a DAR name. Nicholas Cox was never a governor, although he played a very active role as a soldier and builder in the area.

GRAND PRE: Annapolis Valley town, famous Acadian village, and home of Longfellow's Evangeline.

GRANDFONTAINE: Chevalier de Grandfontaine, governor of Acadia 1670–1678.

HALIBURTON: Thomas Chandler Haliburton, Nova Scotia judge and author who created Sam Slick and the Clockmaker series.

HALIFAX: Nova Scotia capital named for the Earl of Halifax, George Montague, who presided over the British Board of Trade, which directed the earliest development of the city.

HEBERT: Louis Hébert, an apothecary, has been described as the first true settler in Canada because his family accompanied him to Nova Scotia.

HIAWATHA: Lead figure in another of Longfellow's epic poems, *Song of Hiawatha.*

HOWE: Joseph Howe, premier and lieutenant-governor Nova Scotia, newspaper owner, and early railway advocate.

KENT: Father of Queen Victoria and commander-in-chief of the British forces in North America.

KENTVILLE: King's county shiretown, headquarters of the W&AR and later the DAR.

LATOUR: Charles de la Tour, French aristocrat, appointed governor of *Acadie*, 1631–42 and 1653–57.

LESCARBOT: Marc Lescarbot, lawyer, writer, naturalist, and historian at Port Royal; author of the *History of New France*.

MASCARENE: Jean Paul Mascarene, British governor of Nova Scotia in the mid-1700s.

MINNEHAHA: Fictional Native American woman in Longfellow's poem *Song of Hiawatha*.

MEMBERTOU: Grand chief of the Mi'kmaq; aided the French at Port Royal.

MOUNT DENSON: Annapolis Valley town.

NICHOLSON: Colonel Francis Nicholson commanded the fleet that defeated the French in *Acadie* and renamed Port Royal as Annapolis; second British governor in Nova Scotia.

OBERON: Shakespearean figure, king of the fairies.

PIONEER: A tribute to the early settlers along the Midland route.

PONTGRAVE: Sieur de Pontgrave, pioneer with the Champlain expedition and tasked with building Habitation at Port Royal.

POUTRINCOURT: Co-founder of Port Royal, succeeded de Monts, became the second governor of Acadia.

PRESIDENT: Used as a name but the reference is not obvious.

QUEEN MAB: Shakespearean figure, a fairy.

REGINA: Latin, meaning "queen."

SAVARY: Alfred Savary was a jurist, statesman, historian, member of Canada's first Parliament, and led the movement to preserve Fort Anne.

ST. EULALIE: Referred to in Longfellow's *Evangeline*.

STRATHCONA: Donald Smith, Lord Strathcona, key figure in the building of the CPR.

SUBERCASE: Daniel d'Auger de Subercase, last Governor of *Acadie*.

TITANIA: Shakespearean figure, queen of the fairies.

TRURO: Central Nova Scotia town, northern terminus of the Midland Railway; pre-existed the Empire Loyalists; uncertainty as to the source of the name.

VALLIERE: Sieur de la Vallière, successor to Grandfontaine as governor of *Acadie*.

VILLEBON: Sieur de Villebon recaptured *Acadie* for the French in 1690.

WESTERN: Derived from the name of the WCR.

WEYMOUTH: Nova Scotia town founded by Empire Loyalists; named in honour of one of the founding families, the Stricklands, whose previous home was Weymouth, Massachusetts.

WINDSOR: Annapolis Valley town at the southern terminus of the Midland Railway.

YARMOUTH: Western Nova Scotia town; the western terminus of the DAR.

Sources: *Highlights of Nova Scotia History* (DAR booklet), Omer Lavallée's 1985 *Canadian Pacific Steam Locomotives*, J. B. King articles, and Marguerite Woodworth's 1936 *History of the Dominion Atlantic Railway*.

INDEX

numbers in italics refer to images